Table of Contents

Want to be Wise AF?

50 timeless principles to guide you through life
real-world examples

Jason McKesson

The Wise AF Principles

1. The Golden Rule: treat others as you would want to be treated.
2. How you do one thing is how you do everything.
3. "Observation without evaluation is the highest form of human intelligence" (Jiddu Krishnamurti).
4. "Hard choices, easy life. Easy choices, hard life" (Jerzy Gregorek).
5. "Movement is life" (Aristotle).
6. Control what you can control.
7. Wake up early.
8. Put first things first.
9. Time kills deals.
10. Listen to your body.
11. Be a problem solver.
12. If one way does not work, what are you doing differently?
13. "First seek to understand, then to be understood" (Stephen R. Covey).
14. Everything in moderation.
15. Spend time with friends and/or family at least once per week.
16. Catch up on current events at least once per week.
17. Embrace the struggle.
18. Use acute pain to diffuse the constant pain.
19. A lie is usually seen, rarely heard.
20. Everything you want is on the other side of fear.
21. Always try your best.

22. Find your peak time and tackle your most important tasks then.
23. Fear has a voice but not a vote.
24. Think win-win.
25. We sink to the level of our systems.
26. "Great opportunities never have 'great opportunity' in the subject line" (Scott Belsky).
27. "He suffers more than necessary who suffers before it is necessary" (Seneca the Younger).
28. Use energy like you use electricity: intelligently.
29. Choose a growth mindset, not a fixed one.
30. If a dog bites you once, it's the dog's fault. If a dog bites you twice, it's your fault.
31. Resistance is most powerful at the finish line.
32. Always contemplate how you can turn a negative situation into a positive one.
33. Always have something to look forward to in life.
34. Regular quiet time fuels motivation.
35. Practice gratitude: be grateful for the positives in your life.
36. Find the fire that motivates you.
37. Life's greatest opportunities run on their own schedule.
38. Epiphanies happen either when you switch off or by the dissent of others.
39. "What you seek is seeking you." (Rumi)
40. You have to be good every day to be great.
41. If you're not going forward, then you're going backward.
42. In order to be a level 10 person, you must be at a level 10 in personal development.
43. Find a mentor.
44. When engaging with others, always give a compliment or say something positive.

45. Trust your gut.
46. Seize the moment.
47. Have empathy and give people grace: everyone is going through something.
48. Learn how to motivate others.
49. Progress every day.
50. Be proactive.

Introduction

I have always been an observer first and a doer second. I like to sit back, watch, read the room, and then act. The wisdom in this book didn't come from theory or textbooks. It came from paying attention, making mistakes, getting back up, and trying again. These aren't hacks. They're life principles. When you live by them consistently, they help you move through life like you actually know what you're doing. You may notice some overlap in some of the lessons. That is intentional, as many of the tactics mentioned relate to more than one principle. My hope is that at least some of these principles can help lead you to success in your life as they did in mine and in those of countless others who live by them.

—Jason McKesson

The Golden Rule: Treat Others as You Would Want to Be Treated

IN TODAY'S fast-moving world, where so many interactions feel quick and transactional, choosing to really step into someone else's shoes can make all the difference. When we take the time to approach others with empathy and care, we create relationships that feel real and trustworthy. That effort often sparks a ripple effect. Kindness inspires kindness, easing tension and opening the door to collaboration. Over time, this practice strengthens both personal and professional bonds and helps build a culture of respect. By treating others with the same thoughtfulness we'd hope to receive, we create spaces where everyone can thrive.

How to Implement This in Your Life

- **Practice active listening.** When talking with others, make a conscious effort to truly hear their perspectives, concerns, and needs. Hold back from interrupting, and focus on understanding where they're coming from.

- **Communicate with empathy and kindness.** Choose words that are clear and caring. Aim to share your message in a way that feels respectful and supportive while steering clear of harsh tones, sarcasm, or put-downs.
- **Offer help and support.** Look for moments to lend a hand, whether it's helping a co-worker with a project, being there for a friend in a tough time, or offering kindness to a stranger. Imagine how you'd want support, and act from that place.
- **Handle conflicts with compassion.** When disagreements come up, approach them with curiosity and problem-solving rather than defensiveness. Focus on finding solutions that work for everyone involved.
- **Extend grace and forgiveness.** Remember that everyone slips up sometimes. When someone disappoints you, think about how you'd hope to be treated in their shoes. Offer that same grace and understanding.
- **Celebrate the success of others.** Take genuine joy in the wins of the people around you. A heartfelt "congratulations" or acknowledgment goes a long way and creates connection.
- **Lead by example.** Show up with the respect and consideration you'd like to see in the world. Your behavior can influence and inspire those around you more than you might realize.
- **Reflect with self-awareness.** Check in with yourself often. How are you using your words, your tone, and your actions? Ask if they reflect how you'd want to be treated. Use these reflections to guide your growth.

Real-World Example

Back in 2013, Katie Bouman was a graduate student with a bold goal: to help capture the very first image of a black hole.[1] The project's scope was daunting. It required assembling data from telescopes scattered across the globe and weaving together contributions from astronomers, engineers, and computer scientists. The technical hurdles alone would have been enough to discourage most, but Katie recognized that the human element mattered just as much as the science.

She made a conscious effort to cultivate trust within the group. Instead of pushing only her own ideas, Katie emphasized collaboration. She took time to listen carefully to colleagues with very different backgrounds and areas of expertise. She encouraged open dialogue, invited multiple perspectives, and reinforced the idea that every contribution, no matter how small it might appear, was essential to the overall mission. In doing so, she turned what could have been an intimidating, high-pressure environment into one where people felt supported and empowered.

Katie also practiced giving feedback in a way that motivated rather than discouraged. By highlighting what was working before offering suggestions for improvement, she ensured her teammates felt respected and valued. Her approach built resilience in the team. When inevitable setbacks occurred, members felt more willing to push forward rather than retreat into frustration. That sense of inclusion and mutual respect

---

[1] Sarah Mervosh. "Katie Bouman: The Woman Behind the First Black Hole Image." *The New York Times.* April 11, 2019. https://www.nytimes.com/2019/04/11/science/katie-bouman-black-hole.html.

became a binding force that kept the group united through years of meticulous work.

The results spoke for themselves. In 2019, after years of patient coordination and countless hours of effort, the Event Horizon Telescope collaboration unveiled the now-famous image of the black hole at the center of galaxy M87.[2] It was a breakthrough that captured worldwide attention, not only for its scientific significance but also as a testament to the power of teamwork. At the center of that story was Katie's example: treating others with empathy and fairness (how she would want to be treated), and showing that great discoveries are rarely the product of individual brilliance alone, but of communities built on trust and respect.

---

[2] Sarah Kaplan. "Meet Katie Bouman, One Woman Who Helped Make the World's First Black Hole Image." *The Washington Post*. April 10, 2019. https://www.washingtonpost.com/science/2019/04/10/ see-black-hole-first-time-images-event-horizon-telescope/.

2

How You Do One Thing Is How You Do Everything

THIS PRINCIPLE reminds us that our habits and behaviors are all connected, no matter which part of life we're talking about. This is powerful because it pushes us to be more self-aware and consistent in how we show up. When we notice patterns in one area (like procrastinating on work), we often see the same habits spill into other areas, such as putting off tough conversations or delaying important choices. By addressing those patterns at the root, we can create positive change across many areas of our lives. Building good habits in one area, like committing to daily exercise, can naturally strengthen other areas, such as how we manage money or stay on top of deadlines. When we live with this mindset, we become more efficient, less stressed, and more balanced overall. Instead of treating challenges as separate issues, we create a more fulfilling, connected approach to growth.[3]

---

[3] T. Harv Eker, *Secrets of the Millionaire Mind: Mastering the Inner Game of Wealth* (New York: HarperBusiness, 2005).

How to Implement This in Your Life

- **Check in with yourself regularly.** Take time to reflect on your habits across different parts of your life, such as work, health, relationships, and personal growth. Look for patterns that repeat, and notice where you're consistent (or not).
- **Build steady routines.** Create daily or weekly practices that you carry out with the same level of care, whether it's your morning routine, your workouts, or the way you handle tasks at work.
- **Give equal effort to big and small tasks.** Treat every task with the same level of focus and commitment, no matter how minor it seems. Avoid cutting corners. Doing so will allow you to build trust in yourself and with others.
- **Stay mindful and present.** Be intentional about how you show up in each moment. Whether it's something ordinary or a big milestone, bring the same awareness and energy.
- **Ask for feedback.** Invite honest input from friends, family, or mentors about the consistency they see in your actions. Use their perspective to learn and grow.
- **Celebrate your wins.** Recognize and reward yourself for small moments where you put this principle into practice. Celebrating even the little things helps keep the momentum going.

A Real-World Example

Early in her career, Oprah Winfrey approached every interview with the same preparation and respect, whether she was talking with someone unknown or a famous guest. She never treated one conversation as more important than another. That consistency quickly became her hallmark, helping her earn the trust of both audiences and colleagues. People could sense that she was genuinely interested in their stories, not just in creating a flashy moment for television. That level of care built a foundation of credibility that carried her from local news to a national stage.

What set Oprah apart was her ability to show up fully, no matter the circumstance. She prepared diligently, asked thoughtful questions, and treated each guest with dignity. Over time, that approach created a sense of intimacy with viewers. Millions felt as if she was talking directly to them. By honoring every opportunity with the same level of attention, she demonstrated that excellence doesn't come from waiting for the "big break," but from consistently bringing your best to whatever is in front of you.

Later, she carried that same commitment into her talk show, her productions, and her philanthropy.[4] The same principles that guided her during those early interviews shaped how she built her company, selected projects, and engaged in giving back. She didn't compartmentalize her effort. Her work, her leadership, and her generosity were all infused with the same sense of purpose and care.

---

[4] Oprah Winfrey, *The Path Made Clear: Discovering Your Life's Direction and Purpose* (New York: Flatiron Books, 2019).

Her story is a reminder that bringing the same dedication to everything we do, whether the task seems small or monumental, can create lasting success. Even the most influential figures began by showing up consistently in ordinary moments. Oprah's journey illustrates that when we put our full effort into each opportunity, we not only shape our reputation but also create momentum that carries us toward even greater achievements.

3

"Observation without Evaluation Is the Highest Form of Human Intelligence" (Jiddu Krishnamurti)[5]

IT'S EASY to rush to conclusions. We all do it. Our brains are wired to make snap judgments to simplify the world around us. However, something powerful happens when we slow down and simply observe. When we let go of labeling or evaluating everything we see, we give ourselves a chance to understand things more fully. Whether it's a situation, a conversation, or even our own emotions, creating that pause allows us to see with fresh eyes, without the fog of assumptions or bias.

This kind of presence builds empathy. It helps us truly hear other people as opposed to waiting for our turn to talk. It

---

5 Jiddu Krishnamurti, *The First and Last Freedom* (San Francisco: Harper, 1954), 219.

makes our relationships stronger, our decisions wiser, and our inner lives a little clearer.

How to Implement This in Your Life

- **Practice active listening.** Instead of mentally drafting your reply while someone else is talking, try to be fully present. Tune into their words, tone, and emotion.
- **Pause before reacting.** When something pushes your buttons, take a breath. Notice the feeling, but don't let it drive your response immediately.
- **Write it out.** Journaling your day without judgment (just noting what happened and how you felt) can offer surprising insights over time.
- **Let go of being "right."** Especially in disagreements, resist the urge to win. Choose to understand instead. You might learn something new.
- **Get mindful.** Meditation or just a quiet moment each day can help train your brain to notice without reacting.

Real-World Example

One of the most powerful examples of this in action was Dr. Martin Luther King Jr. during the Birmingham civil rights protests in 1963. The atmosphere at the time was filled with hostility, fear, and constant injustice. Many leaders in his position might have answered that pressure with anger or retaliation, but Dr. King chose a different path. He refused to let the bitterness of the moment dictate his response. Instead, he listened. He listened to those who doubted him and even to those who openly opposed him.

That willingness to hear every voice shaped the way he carried himself during those critical days. By taking in different perspectives, he was able to frame his arguments with both clarity and compassion. The result was one of the most influential pieces of writing of the twentieth century: his "Letter from Birmingham Jail." Written in the most difficult of circumstances, the letter did not erupt with rage or hostility. It was measured, thoughtful, and filled with a moral clarity that spoke far beyond the walls of the jail cell.[6]

Dr. King used reason to challenge his critics and compassion to call them higher. His words reached across divides, helping people who might never have seen the struggle up close understand the urgency of the cause. In choosing patience and empathy, he gave the movement a voice that was strong without being harsh and firm without being cruel.

His words moved a nation. His example continues to remind us that listening deeply and responding with respect can turn even the most painful conflicts into opportunities for understanding and change.

---

[6] Martin Luther King Jr., *Why We Can't Wait* (New York: Harper & Row, 1964).

4

"Hard Choices, Easy Life. Easy Choices, Hard Life" (Jerzy Gregorek)[7]

THIS QUOTE hits home, doesn't it? On the surface, it's simple, but the truth behind it is deep. The easy road is tempting. It feels safe, comfortable, and stress-free . . . for now. However, over time, those easy choices, such as avoiding responsibility, pushing off growth, and ignoring what we know we need to face, can lead to harder outcomes down the line.

On the other hand, when we have the courage to make the tough calls early on, life tends to reward us later. Choose discipline over distraction, honesty over comfort, and action over procrastination. That's where real progress lives.

---

[7] Jerzy Gregorek and Aniela Gregorek. *The Happy Body: The Simple Science of Nutrition, Exercise, and Relaxation.* (Los Altos, CA: Jurania Press, 2010).

How to Implement This in Your Life

- **Personal growth.** It's easy to stay comfortable, but growth comes from leaning into discomfort by learning the skill, facing the fear, or breaking the habit. That's where confidence starts.
- **Money matters.** Swiping the card is easy. Sticking to a budget and saving? Not so much. But the peace of financial stability is worth every bit of that effort.
- **Health.** Burgers and binge-watching are fun. But long-term wellness comes from daily decisions like moving your body, fueling it right, and getting enough rest.
- **Relationships.** Skipping hard conversations or settling for surface-level connections might feel easier in the moment. However, true connection takes vulnerability, boundaries, and communication.
- **Doing the right thing.** Sometimes, the right path is the hardest one. It might not be convenient, but choosing integrity over shortcuts builds self-respect that no one can take away.

Real-World Example

David Goggins is a real-life example of what it looks like to choose the hard path and reap the long-term rewards. His early life was filled with pain, poverty, and self-doubt. For years he felt stuck, weighed down by the environment around him and by the belief that nothing better was possible. In those days, comfort looked like giving up before he even tried. In fact, for a while he stayed there, taking the path of least resistance and settling for less than he was capable of.

But one day, he had had enough. He decided that the life he was living was no longer acceptable. That turning point led him to make a bold decision: to train for the Navy SEALs, one of the most grueling and demanding paths a person can attempt.[8] The training pushed him past every physical and mental limit he thought he had. He failed more than once, but each time, he got back up. He battled through injuries, exhaustion, and the constant voice in his head telling him to quit. Every setback became an opportunity to push further, and every challenge became a test of how much he was willing to endure.

Becoming a SEAL was not the end of his journey, but the foundation for what came next. Goggins continued to search for new ways to challenge himself. He went on to conquer ultramarathons, take on extreme endurance events, and even set world records in feats of strength and stamina.[9] None of it came because the road was smooth or because the obstacles disappeared. Each accomplishment was the result of deliberately choosing the hard road, again and again, when the easier option was right there in front of him.

He made sure to share his lessons. His story has inspired millions of people around the world by proving that struggle can become a springboard to success. Goggins shows us that when we deliberately lean into difficulty instead of avoiding it, we build toughness, discipline, and a deeper belief in our own potential. Each choice to grow instead of retreat creates a stronger version of ourselves, one that is better equipped to face whatever life brings.

---

[8] David Goggins, *Can't Hurt Me: Master Your Mind and Defy the Odds* (New York: Lioncrest Publishing, 2018), 53–75.

[9] Ibid., 201–230.

5

"Movement Is Life" (Aristotle)[10]

"MOVEMENT IS life," is a simple phrase, but, wow, does it carry weight. Movement isn't just about hitting the gym or going for a jog (although that helps too). It's about forward motion in every part of our lives—body, mind, heart, and spirit. When we stop moving, we stagnate. When we keep showing up, staying curious, and pushing ourselves, life starts to open up.

How to Implement This in Your Life

- **Move your body.** Aim for forty-five minutes of activity three times a week. Walk, dance, lift, or stretch (whatever makes you feel alive). You don't have to crush a marathon; just start where you are.

---

[10] Aristotle, *De Anima*, trans. Hugh Lawson-Tancred (London: Penguin Classics, 1987).

- **Keep learning.** Read, explore new ideas, take a class, or just ask more questions. Keeping your mind active keeps life interesting.
- **Lean into change.** Growth can be messy. Saying "yes" to new experiences helps you evolve and stay flexible in the face of challenges.
- **Chase your goals.** Big or small, keep moving toward something that matters to you. Progress doesn't have to be perfect; it just has to be forward.

Real-World Example

Before the world knew Harry Potter, J. K. Rowling was a struggling single mom writing in cafés and trying simply to stay afloat. Her life at that point was far from glamorous. She had bills to pay, a child to care for, and little certainty about what tomorrow might look like. Yet in the middle of that uncertainty, she clung to the small pocket of time she had to create. With a cup of coffee at her side, she poured words onto the page, building a world that only she could see at first.

It was not an easy road. She faced rejection after rejection from publishers.[11] Each letter telling her "no" could have been the excuse to put her dream away for good, but she refused to let those setbacks silence her. Instead, she treated every rejection as part of the process. She went back to her manuscript, revised it again, and looked for another chance. That cycle repeated more times than most people would have endured. Still, she kept showing up.

---

[11] Sean Smith, *J. K. Rowling: A Biography* (London: Arrow Books, 2001).

Every coffee-fueled writing session mattered. Every "no" that she turned into a new draft was movement. The world had not yet caught up to her vision, but she kept moving forward anyway. That persistence carried her through the fog of doubt. She chose to believe that progress, however small, was better than standing still. Over time, those ordinary days of writing in cafés became the foundation of something extraordinary.

Eventually, that movement led to one of the most beloved stories of all time. Harry Potter did not appear overnight. It grew from years of steady effort, thousands of handwritten pages, and a determination to keep going when it would have been easier to quit. Rowling's journey is a powerful reminder that momentum does not come from perfect circumstances but from the decision to keep stepping forward.

When life feels heavy, take one step, then another. Even when the path is uncertain, movement keeps hope alive. With hope comes the possibility that what feels impossible today might just become the success story of tomorrow.

6

Control What You Can Control

LET'S BE honest, life throws curveballs. Some things are out of your hands, no matter how much you care or try. Here's the game-changer: you don't have to control everything to feel empowered. When you focus your energy on the things you *can* influence (your actions, mindset, and habits), you shift from feeling helpless to feeling capable.

This mindset is about making peace with the chaos around you and choosing where to plant your effort. Instead of spiraling over what-ifs or other people's opinions, you stay anchored in your power. Over time, this leads to more confidence, resilience, and clarity (especially during tough times).

Plus, it helps your mental health. Worrying about things you can't change is exhausting. By letting go of the uncontrollable, you free up your mind to be calm, present, and productive. You start solving problems instead of just stressing about them.

How to Implement This in Your Life

- **Direct your focus wisely.** When something's bothering you, pause and ask: "Is this within my control?" If it's not, release it. Put your energy where it can make a difference.
- **Ease stress and worry.** Catch yourself when you're ruminating. Interrupt that loop with a deep breath and the reminder: "This isn't mine to carry."
- **Make decisions with clarity.** Clear away the distractions of what you *can't* change, and suddenly, your next step becomes more obvious.
- **Own your actions.** What you say and do is up to you. That's powerful. When you take full responsibility for how you show up, you naturally grow into someone others can count on and someone *you* can be proud of.
- **Adapt when life shifts.** Life doesn't always go to plan. But you can pivot, adjust, and keep moving. That's where strength is built.
- **Grow through intentional effort.** Put consistent effort into the things within your control: your habits, health, and learning. These are the building blocks of long-term success.

Real-World Example

At the 2008 Beijing Olympics, Michael Phelps was chasing history, aiming for eight gold medals in a single Olympic Games. The pressure was enormous. Every race was watched by millions of people around the world, and every stroke brought him closer to something no one had ever done before. In the middle of that pressure cooker, during the 200-meter butterfly final, disaster struck. As soon as he dove in, his goggles began to leak. By the time he hit the water for the final laps, they were completely filled. He could not see the wall, the lane, or his competitors.

In a moment like that, most athletes would have unraveled. Losing sight in the middle of an Olympic final could easily lead to panic, a broken rhythm, or the collapse of months of preparation. Phelps chose a different response. Instead of letting fear take over, he leaned on the one thing he had built through endless hours in the pool: trust in his training. He focused on what he could control. He counted his strokes, stayed steady with his breathing, and kept his composure even as the world blurred around him.

Every practice leading up to Beijing had taught him how to rely on fundamentals when conditions were less than perfect. He had trained in ways that pushed him beyond comfort, rehearsed difficult scenarios, and built habits that would carry him through when things went wrong. In that moment, when the unexpected happened, he did not need to invent a new strategy. He simply executed what he already knew.

Not only did he win the race, but he also claimed that record-breaking eighth gold medal, cementing his place in Olympic history.[12] The victory was not just about physical strength, but about the mental discipline to stay calm under pressure. It showed that greatness often comes from choosing focus over fear, and control over chaos.

---

[12] Michael Phelps and Alan Abrahamson, *No Limits: The Will to Succeed* (New York: Free Press, 2008), 96–98.

Let that be your reminder. You cannot control everything that happens to you, but you can always control how you respond. Your reaction, your mindset, and your ability to keep moving forward are your greatest superpowers.

7

Wake Up Early

THERE'S SOMETHING magical about the quiet of the early morning. There are no buzzing phones, emails, or reasons to rush. There is just space to breathe, think, and move with intention. Waking up early gives you a head start not just on your to-do list, but on your mindset. You create time for yourself before the world starts demanding your attention.

Whether you're knocking out a workout, planning your day, or simply sipping your coffee in peace, those early hours can become sacred. It's not about being a morning person, but about reclaiming your time and setting the tone for how you want your day to unfold.

How to Implement This in Your Life

- **Choose a time and stick to it.** Whether it's 6:00 a.m. or earlier, commit to that wake-up time (even on weekends). Your body and mind will adjust, and the consistency will make mornings easier over time.

22

- **Prep the night before.** Make your mornings smooth and stress-free. Lay out your clothes, prep your meals, and charge your devices (anything that helps you wake up with less friction).
- **Protect your sleep.** Early mornings only work if you're well rested. Aim for seven to eight hours of sleep. That means adjusting your bedtime and treating sleep like the priority it is.
- **Create a morning flow.** Give yourself something to look forward to, such as journaling, a workout, meditation, or just a peaceful cup of tea. A consistent ritual builds momentum.
- **Celebrate small wins.** Did you get up early for a full week? Treat yourself! Whether it's a new book, a favorite breakfast, or a walk in the sunshine, be sure to acknowledge your effort.
- **Stick with it.** Changing sleep habits takes time. There'll be days when it's tough. That's normal. Keep going. You're building something powerful.

Real-World Example

Apple CEO Tim Cook is famous for rising early to start his day. He reportedly wakes up at around 4:00 a.m. each morning.[13] His early start gives him precious quiet time before the chaos begins. It gives him time to focus, move, and think clearly.

---

[13] Adam Lashinsky, *Inside Apple: How America's Most Admired—and Secretive—Company Really Works* (New York: Business Plus, 2012).

He uses those early hours to exercise, clear emails, and lay out his priorities.[14] But what really stands out is how he's turned this habit into a strategic advantage. During high-pressure moments, like preparing for major Apple product launches, those quiet early hours allow him to review performance data, coordinate across time zones, and stay grounded under pressure.

It's not about hustle for hustle's sake. It is about focus, discipline, and making time for what truly matters. Cook's commitment to early rising has become part of his leadership identity and a key ingredient in Apple's continued success.

His story reminds us that the early hours are often where the most important moves are made. Imagine what you could accomplish if you consistently claimed that time for yourself.

---

[14] Nick Hobson. "Up at 3:45 a.m., in Bed by 8:45 p.m.: How Apple's CEO Tim Cook Uses Energy Rituals to Optimize His Life." *Inc.* July 4, 2022, https://www.inc.com/nick-hobson/up-at-345am-in-bed-by-845pm-how-apples-ceo-tim-cook-uses-energy-rituals-to-optimize-his-life.html.

8

Put First Things First

IT'S EASY to get caught up in the whirlwind of everyday life. Every day we're bombarded with emails, errands, and endless to-do lists. When you stop and really look at how you're spending your time, are you focused on what matters most?

Putting first things first is about being intentional. It's about identifying the priorities that truly move your life forward (like your health, your relationships, and your goals) and giving them the time and energy they deserve. It's not about doing more, but about doing what matters.[15]

How to Implement This in Your Life

- **Identify your priorities**. Pause and reflect: What really matters to you? Family? Health? Career

---

[15] Stephen R. Covey, *The 7 Habits of Highly Effective People* (New York: Free Press, 1989).

growth? Make a list and rank them. These are your "first things."

- **Build a schedule around what matters**. Block time in your calendar for the things that support your top priorities. Whether it's a workout, time with loved ones, or deep work, treat it like it's non-negotiable.
- **Learn to say no.** You don't have to say yes to everything. Protect your time. If something doesn't align with your priorities, kindly decline. "No" is a complete sentence.
- **Cut the noise**. Distractions are everywhere, from your phone, to notifications, to social media. Set boundaries. Create focused time where you can truly engage with what matters.
- **Take care of yourself**. Self-care isn't selfish; it's fuel. Prioritize sleep, movement, and moments that recharge you. A clear mind and energized body will help you show up for what matters.
- **Review and adjust regularly**. Life changes. Priorities shift. Check in with yourself weekly or monthly and ask, "Am I still aligned with what's most important?"
- **Delegate and let go**. Not everything has to be on your plate. Ask for help. Share the load. Focus on where your energy makes the biggest difference.
- **Find accountability**. Surround yourself with people who support your priorities. Share your goals. Ask a friend to check in, or join a group that keeps you on track.

Real-World Example

When Steve Jobs rejoined Apple in 1997, the company was struggling. It had a bloated product lineup, and many of its offerings weren't resonating with consumers. Apple was trying to be everything to everyone, and it was losing its identity.[16]

Jobs came back with a clear message: simplify and focus. Instead of trying to fix every product or project at once, he asked one simple but powerful question: "What matters most?" He quickly slashed the product line, cutting it down to just four main categories: a consumer desktop, a professional desktop, a consumer laptop, and a professional laptop.[17]

This radical focus allowed Apple to pour its resources and energy into doing fewer things better. The result was the iMac, a sleek, innovative, all-in-one computer that made a huge splash in 1998.[18] It wasn't just a new product; it was a bold statement that Apple was back, and it was focused.

Jobs's commitment to putting first things first and choosing clarity over clutter reignited Apple's creative spark. That single shift laid the foundation for future successes like the iPod, iPhone, and iPad. Instead of spreading thin, Apple leaned in.

---

[16] Walter Isaacson, *Steve Jobs* (New York: Simon & Schuster, 2011), 343–45.

[17] Ibid.

[18] Brent Schlender and Rick Tetzeli, *Becoming Steve Jobs: The Evolution of a Reckless Upstart into a Visionary Leader* (New York: Crown Currency, 2015), 268–72.

His story reminds us that when you focus on the few things that matter most, you create space for excellence. Jobs didn't just rebuild a company, but reshaped an industry. Most importantly, it all started with deciding what truly deserved his team's attention.

9

Time Kills Deals

"TIME KILLS deals" is a phrase often tossed around in business, but it applies far beyond boardrooms and negotiations. At its core, it's a reminder that hesitation and delay can quietly sabotage progress. Opportunities don't wait. They evolve, disappear, or get picked up by someone else. Whether it's a new job, a business venture, or even a relationship, acting with urgency can make the difference between moving forward and missing out.

This doesn't mean being reckless. It means being decisive. It means trusting your instincts, gathering just enough information to make a smart choice, and then moving. When you develop the habit of acting with purpose, you open more doors and close more deals.

How to Implement This in Your Life

- **Make decisions faster**. When you're stuck in indecision, ask: "What happens if I do nothing?"

Use that urgency to guide you toward thoughtful, timely action.

- **Set time-bound goals**. Give your goals deadlines and act on them consistently. Don't wait for perfect conditions, as they rarely come. Progress beats perfection.
- **Move with intention in conversations**. In deals, tough talks, or everyday exchanges, know when the window is open and don't be afraid to act. Timing is often more important than getting every detail perfect.
- **Jump on opportunities**. See something exciting like a job lead, mentor, or chance to invest or grow? Evaluate it quickly and take the first step. Too much waiting can mean never starting at all.
- **Use the phrase as a mental trigger**. The next time you catch yourself procrastinating, whisper it: "Time kills deals." Let it pull you back into motion.
- **Stay agile**. Plans change. Life shifts. The quicker you can adapt and take action, the more likely you are to stay ahead of the curve and the competition.

Real-World Example

Warren Buffett is known for his patience, but he also knows when not to wait. A great example? His legendary investment in GEICO. Back in the mid-1970s, GEICO was in trouble. The company was struggling financially, and most investors were steering clear. It looked risky.

Buffett saw something different in GEICO. He believed in the company's potential and didn't let fear or indecision slow him down. While others hesitated, he acted. He began buying shares aggressively, even while the company was still navigating uncertainty.[19]

This wasn't just luck. Buffett had studied GEICO for years. He trusted the fundamentals, understood the leadership potential, and knew the window wouldn't stay open forever. His quick action secured a major stake in the company before its rebound. Over the years, GEICO became one of Berkshire Hathaway's most successful investments.[20]

Buffett's move is a masterclass in timing. He didn't wait for a perfect moment. He recognized a rare opportunity and moved decisively. It's a powerful reminder that when you see something worth pursuing, acting quickly (and smartly) can lead to extraordinary outcomes. Time, after all, really does kill deals.

---

[19] Roger Lowenstein, *Buffett: The Making of an American Capitalist* (New York: Random House, 1995), 236–238.
[20] Alice Schroeder, *The Snowball: Warren Buffett and the Business of Life* (New York: Bantam Books, 2008), 404–406.

10

Listen to Your Body

YOUR BODY is always speaking to you. It's just a matter of whether you're paying attention. Sometimes it whispers through low energy or tension. Other times, it shouts through pain or burnout. Learning to listen to these signals isn't just about health; it's about self-respect.

Tuning in to your body can help you make smarter decisions, reduce stress, and move through life with more ease. When you're aligned with your body's needs, you naturally become more grounded, mindful, and resilient. It's not about being perfect. It's about checking in, adjusting when needed, and treating yourself with care.

How to Implement This in Your Life

- **Develop body awareness.** Throughout your day, notice how you feel physically. Are your shoulders tense? Are you dragging your feet? These cues tell a story. Learn to listen.

32

- **Do regular check-ins.** Pause now and then to scan your body. Take a few deep breaths and ask yourself, "How am I feeling right now?" You'll catch things early, before they turn into problems.
- **Respond when your body speaks.** Feeling worn out? Rest. Stomach growling? Eat something nourishing. Ignoring signals often leads to bigger issues, so respect your body's voice.
- **Adjust your habits.** Use what your body tells you to fine-tune your routines. Perhaps that means a gentler workout, a more consistent sleep schedule, or a shift in your diet.
- **Practice mindfulness.** Meditation, yoga, or body scan exercises can help you tune into the present moment and deepen your connection to your physical self.
- **Keep a journal.** Track how you feel after meals, workouts, or stressful days. Patterns will emerge, and you'll get better at predicting and managing your needs.
- **Seek help when needed.** If something feels off and you're unsure why, reach out to a healthcare provider. Listening to your body also means knowing when to ask for support.

Real-World Example

In 2011, tennis legend Serena Williams faced a terrifying health scare. After experiencing shortness of breath and swelling in her legs, she initially brushed it off as exhaustion from training. However, something didn't feel right. She listened to that inner voice—and it saved her life.[21]

Medical tests revealed a pulmonary embolism: a serious, potentially fatal condition involving blood clots in the lungs. Instead of pushing through, Serena made the tough but necessary choice to pause and prioritize her health. She took time off to heal, mentally and physically.[22]

This decision wasn't easy. For someone driven by fierce competition and a relentless desire to win, slowing down felt foreign. This experience reshaped how she approached her career and her well-being.

When she returned to the court in 2012, she came back stronger, in both skill and balance. That year, she won both Wimbledon and the US Open.[23] More importantly, she had learned how to lead with intuition and self-awareness.

Serena's story is a powerful reminder that our bodies often know what our minds try to ignore. Listening isn't weakness. It's wisdom. Sometimes, it's the most important decision you'll ever make.

---

[21] Mike Henson. "Wimbledon 2012: Serena Williams Wins Fifth Singles Title." *BBC*. July 7, 2012. https://www.bbc.com/sport/tennis/18749540.

[22] Christopher Clarey. "In Comebacks, Serena Williams Showed 'You Can Never Underestimate Her.'" *The New York Times*. Sept. 2022. https://www.nytimes.com/2022/08/29/sports/tennis/serena-williams-comebacks-us-open.html.

[23] Liz Clarke. "Serena Williams Outlast Victoria Azarenka to Claim U.S. Opens Women's Title." *The Washington Post*. September 8, 2013. https://www.washingtonpost.com/sports/othersports/serena-williams-outlasts-victoria-azarenka-to-claim-us-open-womens-title/2013/09/08/8c099952-18e5-11e3-a628-7e6dde8f889d_story.html.

11

Be a Problem Solver

LIFE WILL throw problems your way. It's inevitable. Here's the good news: every problem is a doorway to growth if you learn how to walk through it with curiosity, creativity, and courage. When you approach challenges with a problem-solving mindset, you shift from feeling stuck to feeling empowered.

Being a problem solver means you respond with intention. You analyze, adapt, and think ahead. You become more confident under pressure and build a reputation as someone who gets things done.

How to Implement This in Your Life

- **Follow a clear process:** When a problem pops up, try this simple framework:
  1. Define the problem clearly.
  2. Dig into the root cause.
  3. Brainstorm multiple solutions.

35

4. Choose the best option.
5. Put it into action.
6. Measure how it went.
7. If it didn't work, don't give up. Start again and fine-tune your approach until it does.

- **Think ahead.** Don't wait for things to break. Look for ways to improve systems, relationships, or routines before they become problems. Be the person who spots gaps and fills them.
- **Stay curious.** Ask good questions. Learn all you can about the challenge you're facing. The more you understand, the better your solutions will be.
- **Think critically.** Break the problem down into smaller parts, evaluate your options, and think through the possible consequences before you act. Clarity leads to better decisions.
- **See challenges as growth moments.** Instead of feeling defeated by a setback, ask yourself, "What's this trying to teach me?" Every challenge is a skill-building opportunity.
- **Be flexible.** The first solution isn't always the best. Stay open. Adjust. Use what you've got and adapt your plan as needed.
- **Work Well with Others.** Many problems are solved faster and better with a team. Be a great communicator, invite other viewpoints, and collaborate on smart solutions.
- **Learn from What Didn't Work.** Every failure is a chance to refine your approach. Reflect, tweak, and try again. That's how mastery is built.

Real-World Example

Jeff Bezos built a solution machine with Amazon. When Amazon started in the business of selling books, it was about making life easier for customers. With every problem that came up, whether it was slow shipping, limited selection, or frustrating user experiences, Bezos asked one key question: "How do we fix this better than anyone else?"

The answers became some of Amazon's biggest innovations. Amazon Prime tackled shipping delays.[24] The Kindle changed how we read.[25] AWS redefined cloud computing.[26] None of these ideas came from playing it safe. They came from spotting problems and getting bold about solving them.

Bezos didn't do it alone. He built a culture that encouraged problem-solving. Teams were expected to test, fail fast, pivot, and keep their eyes on the long game. Short-term stumbles were acceptable. Long-term value was everything.[27]

His approach turned Amazon into one of the most innovative companies on the planet. More importantly, it proved that when you treat every problem like a creative challenge and keep solving relentlessly, you unlock the kind of results that change industries. That's what being a problem solver is all about.

---

[24] Brad Stone, *The Everything Store: Jeff Bezos and the Age of Amazon* (New York: Little, Brown and Company, 2013), 187–190.

[25] Richard L. Brandt, *One Click: Jeff Bezos and the Rise of Amazon.com* (New York: Portfolio, 2011), 154–157.

[26] John Rossman, *Think Like Amazon: 50 1/2 Ideas to Become a Digital Leader* (New York: McGraw-Hill Education, 2019), 45–48.

[27] Brad Stone, *Amazon Unbound: Jeff Bezos and the Invention of a Global Empire* (New York: Simon & Schuster, 2021), 112–115.

12

If One Way Does Not Work, What Are You Doing Differently?

THIS SIMPLE question can unlock major breakthroughs. It's not just about persistence, but about growth. When you hit a wall, instead of banging your head against it, ask yourself, "What can I do differently?"

Change isn't always easy, but it's often necessary. This mindset reminds you that you don't need to get it right on the first try. What matters is your willingness to adjust, learn, and keep moving. That's how real progress happens.

How to Implement This in Your Life

- **Reflect on what didn't work.** When something falls flat, pause and ask why. Don't just blame yourself. Also analyze your strategy. What could've gone differently? What might you try instead next time?

- **Keep improving.** You don't need to be perfect. You just need to keep evolving. View failure as feedback. Every setback is a lesson in disguise.
- **Get input from others.** Sometimes we're too close to our own problems. Reach out to someone you trust. A mentor, a friend, or a colleague might see something you don't.
- **Try a new angle.** If one plan didn't work, try another. Tweak it. Flip it. Break it into smaller steps. Test different approaches until you find what clicks.
- **Stay flexible.** Plans change. Conditions shift. The more willing you are to adapt, the more resilient and successful you'll be.
- **Apply this everywhere.** This isn't just about work. Try it with your goals, relationships, and routines. Whenever something feels stuck, ask yourself the question—and be open to changing course.

Real-World Example

Thomas Edison didn't just invent the light bulb. He reinvented the way we think about failure. His journey was filled with false starts and failed prototypes. Every single time something didn't work, he changed his approach.

Edison didn't see these failures as dead ends. He saw them as data. Every misstep told him something valuable, such as what materials to avoid, which methods weren't reliable, and where the next idea might be hiding. He kept testing, kept adjusting, and kept learning.

In fact, it took over a thousand tries before he landed on a working design. That kind of persistence is rare, but what's even more powerful is how he kept evolving with each attempt.

He famously said, "I have not failed. I've just found ten thousand ways that won't work."[28] That mindset (the refusal to stay stuck, the willingness to do things differently) is what turned an idea into one of the most important inventions of all time.

[28] B.C. Forbes. *America's 50 Foremost Business Leaders*. New York: B.C. Forbes and Sons, 1948.

13

"First Seek to Understand, Then to Be Understood" (Stephen J. Covey)

THIS PRINCIPLE invites us to slow down our need to be heard and instead lean into understanding others first.[29] It's not always easy. We all want to share our stories, our ideas, and our opinions. However, real connection starts when we choose to listen deeply, not just hear.

When you truly understand where someone else is coming from, everything changes. You open the door to trust, empathy, and meaningful dialogue. Conversations become less about winning and more about connecting. In that space, you're far more likely to be heard when it's your turn to speak.

How to Implement This in Your Life

- **Practice active listening.** Next time you're in a conversation, give your full attention. Don't plan

---

[29] Stephen R. Covey, *The 7 Habits of Highly Effective People: Powerful Lessons in Personal Change* (New York: Free Press, 1989), 235.

your reply, just listen. Ask questions. Reflect back what you've heard to show that you really get it.

- **Hold off on judgment.** Be curious, not critical. Let go of the urge to label or assume. Give people the benefit of the doubt and focus on learning their perspective.
- **Welcome different viewpoints.** Surround yourself with people who think differently. Listen to their stories, struggles, and truths. You'll gain insight and grow your empathy muscle.
- **Reflect on conversations.** After meaningful exchanges, take a moment to think: "What did I learn? Did I listen as much as I spoke? What could I do better next time?"
- **Speak with empathy.** When it's your turn to share, do it with care. Be clear but also kind. Speak in a way that honors the other person's feelings and experience.

Real-World Example

Jay Shetty (author, speaker, and former monk) has built a career around understanding people.[30] That skill didn't just come from books or degrees. It came from years of learning how to truly listen.

During his time in a monastery, Jay wasn't taught to give advice. He was taught to hold space. He was taught stillness, presence, and compassion. Those lessons carried into his life outside the monastery.

---

[30] Jay Shetty, *Think Like a Monk: Train Your Mind for Peace and Purpose Every Day* (New York: Simon & Schuster, 2020), 112–15.

In one of his workshops, Jay met a woman battling anxiety and loneliness. Most people might have jumped in with quick fixes or motivational lines. Jay started by listening.

He asked open-ended questions and let silence do its work. He noticed her tone, her body language, and her pauses. He reflected her words back to her. This was not to correct, but to confirm. He didn't offer advice until he fully understood what she was carrying.

Only then, after she felt seen and safe, did he gently offer tools tailored to her experience. She left the session lighter. This was because someone had *finally* taken the time to understand her.

Jay's approach reminds us that listening is an act of love. When we seek to understand first, we create space for healing, growth, and real connection. Oftentimes, that's exactly what someone needs most.

14

Everything in Moderation

TOO MUCH of anything (no matter how good it seems) can throw your life out of balance. That's where the idea of "everything in moderation" comes in. It's not about depriving yourself or living with strict rules. It's about knowing when enough is enough and learning to enjoy things without going overboard.

This mindset helps you stay grounded. Whether it's your diet, your workload, your screen time, or even your emotions, moderation keeps you from burning out or losing perspective. When you learn to live in the middle instead of the extremes, you create space for peace, stability, and lasting joy.

How to Implement This in Your Life

- **Balance your eating habits.** Eat a variety of nourishing foods, but don't stress over the occasional indulgence. Let your meals reflect both health and enjoyment.

- **Move regularly, and rest fully.** Stay active, but don't push yourself to exhaustion. Mix movement with recovery so your body stays strong *and* resilient.
- **Protect your time.** Work hard, but don't forget to rest and play. Leave room in your day for joy, connection, and relaxation.
- **Keep hobbies healthy.** Love your favorite shows, games, or hobbies? Great! Just don't let them take over. Make sure you're staying engaged with the rest of your life too.
- **Watch your intake.** Whether it's alcohol, caffeine, or screen time, check in with yourself. Ask: "Is this serving me or controlling me?"
- **Regulate emotions with care.** Notice your feelings, but don't let them run the show. Balance means not getting swept up in highs or lows. Create calm within.
- **Think before acting.** Big decisions? Take a breath. Choose the path that reflects your values and long-term vision, not just a quick emotional reaction.
- **Practice healthy boundaries.** In relationships, be present and generous, but not at your own expense. Say yes with love, and no with confidence.

Real-World Example

In 2019, Kevin Hart's life changed in an instant. A serious car accident left him with major spinal injuries and a long road to recovery.[31] Before the crash, Kevin was known for

---

[31] Cheri Mossburg and Marianne Garvey. "Kevin Hart's Wife Says He's 'Going to Be Just Fine.'" *CNN*, September 9, 2019. https://www.cnn.com/2019/09/01/entertainment/kevin-hart-car-crash.

his grind: movie roles, stand-up tours, and nonstop business deals. His hustle was intense. However, it came at a price.

The accident forced him to stop, which was something he rarely did. In those still, painful moments, Kevin began to reflect. He realized that always being "on" had worn him down mentally, emotionally, and spiritually.[32]

During rehab, Kevin prioritized healing over hustling. He committed to physical therapy, cut back on projects, and began choosing work that aligned with his values. He started saying no. He made space for rest, family, and growth.

That shift wasn't easy, but it was transformative. Kevin didn't give up his ambition; he just learned to channel it with balance. He now approaches life with more clarity, more intention, and a deep respect for moderation.

His story is a powerful reminder: success doesn't have to mean sacrificing your well-being. In fact, it's the opposite. The more balanced you are, the more focused, energized, and fulfilled you'll be. Kevin learned that everything in moderation really is the key to a lasting life.

---

[32] Kerry Justich. "Kevin Hart Reflects on How 2019 Car Accident Changed Him." *Yahoo*, January 9, 2023. https://www.yahoo.com/lifestyle/kevin-hart-2019-car-accident-changed-him-213555785.html.

15

Spend Time with Friends and/or Family at Least Once Per Week

LIFE GETS busy. No matter how packed your schedule is, making time for the people you care about is one of the most powerful things you can do for your mental, emotional, and even physical well-being.

Spending time with friends or family just once a week can lift your spirits, reduce stress, and remind you that you're not alone. These moments don't have to be grand or complicated. A simple chat over coffee, a walk in the park, or dinner at home can bring joy, connection, and support that carry you through the week.

How to Implement This in Your Life

- **Put it on the calendar.** Treat your weekly hangout like any other important commitment. Block the time and stick to it.

- **Switch up the setting.** Keep it fresh by rotating locations. You can do one week at home, and the next at a park or your favorite coffee shop.
- **Plan something fun.** Whether it's cooking, playing a game, watching a show, or going for a hike, shared activities deepen bonds.
- **Go digital when needed.** Can't meet in person? A quick video call still counts. Stay connected, even from afar.
- **Make it a family thing.** If you have kids or a partner, get everyone involved. It strengthens family ties and builds shared memories.
- **Stay flexible.** Life happens. If your usual day doesn't work, don't cancel, reschedule. Keep the rhythm going.
- **Protect that time.** Don't let other things bump it off your schedule. This time is about connection, and that's non-negotiable.

Real-World Example

Steph Curry isn't just an NBA superstar. He's also a dedicated family man. Despite his demanding schedule of games, travel, and media commitments, Steph makes a point to carve out time to be with his loved ones.

Even during the busiest stretches of the season, Steph prioritizes family dinners, relaxed evenings at home, or spontaneous outings with his family. He makes sure he is fully engaged in the moment with the people who matter most.

Steph has spoken openly in interviews about how these moments keep him grounded. They remind him of his purpose beyond basketball. That time with his family recharges him, giving him the emotional fuel to navigate the intensity of professional sports.

He doesn't let the spotlight or a packed calendar steal that sacred time. In fact, he's structured his life around protecting it, and it shows. His sense of balance, poise, and gratitude shine through both on and off the court.

Steph's approach proves that no matter how ambitious your goals are, success doesn't have to come at the cost of connection. By consistently investing just a little time into your relationships each week, you build a foundation of love, trust, and joy that supports everything else.

16

Catch Up on Current Events at Least Once Per Week

THE WORLD doesn't stop spinning, and neither should our awareness of it. Staying in the loop with what's going on, whether it's locally, nationally, or globally, can help you feel more connected, better informed, and more prepared to navigate the complexities of modern life.

This habit is about understanding the bigger picture: how global trends affect your community, your work, and your future. It builds empathy, fuels smarter conversations, and helps you make more thoughtful choices in your everyday life.

How to Implement This in Your Life

- **Block time for it.** Choose a consistent time, like Sunday mornings with coffee or during the Friday commute, to catch up on what's happening. Routine makes it stick.

50

- **Pick your go-to sources.** Stick to a few reliable, balanced news outlets. Whether it's a favorite newspaper, podcast, or website, choose what resonates with you and keeps you informed.
- **Switch up the format.** Try articles one week, then a podcast or documentary the next. Mixing formats can keep the experience fresh and fit different parts of your day.
- **Set digital nudges.** Add a recurring calendar reminder or use app alerts to help build the habit. A little nudge can go a long way.

Real-World Example

Malcolm Gladwell (bestselling author and thinker) has long championed the value of staying curious and tuned in. His writing dives into how people, timing, and culture intersect in ways we don't always see.

In his book *Outliers*, Gladwell shows how success isn't just about personal effort, but about understanding the world around you. He highlights how being aware of societal trends, timing, and cultural shifts can offer a powerful edge.[33] This kind of awareness comes from regularly engaging with current events.

Gladwell has talked openly about how consuming news from a variety of sources sharpens his thinking. He listens, reads, and watches across formats and perspectives. This is to gather facts, connect dots, and challenge his own assumptions.

---

[33] Malcolm Gladwell, *Outliers: The Story of Success* (New York: Little, Brown and Company, 2008).

That habit of staying informed helps him spot patterns others miss. It fuels his creativity, his storytelling, and his ability to explain complex ideas in simple, relatable ways. This is something anyone can do.

Following Gladwell's lead means dedicating time each week to learn about what's going on in the world. That's a small habit that can have a big impact on how you think, communicate, and show up in the world around you.

17

Embrace the Struggle

STRUGGLE IS part of life. Instead of running from it, what if we leaned in? Embracing tough moments can shape us in powerful ways. It builds grit, teaches us to problem-solve, and shows us what we're really made of. It deepens our appreciation for the good times and makes us more compassionate toward others who are hurting.

Life won't always be easy, but that doesn't mean it can't be meaningful. When you stop resisting the hard stuff and start seeing it as part of the journey, everything changes. Struggle becomes a teacher rather than a roadblock.

How to Implement This in Your Life

- **Shift how you see challenges.** Stop labeling them as setbacks. Start viewing them as setups for growth.
- **Get comfortable being uncomfortable.** Whether it's a hard conversation or a tough workout, remember that discomfort is where growth begins.

- **Look back and learn.** Keep a journal. Reflect on your struggles and the lessons they've taught you.
- **Be patient with the process.** Growth doesn't happen overnight. Remind yourself that progress often takes time and that's okay.

Real-World Example

When Bethany Hamilton was thirteen, she survived a shark attack that cost her left arm. Most people would've understandably walked away from the sport they loved. Bethany didn't give up. She chose to fight for her passion.[34]

Instead of letting the trauma define her, she learned to surf all over again with one arm. That meant adapting her technique, facing her fears, and pushing through both physical and emotional pain. It wasn't just about getting back on a board, but about rebuilding her confidence and reclaiming her identity.[35]

Bethany didn't pretend the struggle wasn't real. She embraced it. She saw her setback as a setup for something greater. Over time, she became not just a surfer, but a symbol of resilience.[36]

Today, she's still surfing competitively, but she's also inspiring millions through her books, films, and motivational talks.

---

[34] Bethany Hamilton, *Soul Surfer: A True Story of Faith, Family, and Fighting to Get Back on the Board* (New York: MTV Books, 2004).

[35] Aaron Lieber, dir., *Bethany Hamilton: Unstoppable* (Los Angeles: Entertainment Studios Motion Pictures, 2019), documentary film.

[36] Bethany Hamilton, *Body and Soul: A Girl's Guide to a Fit, Fun and Fabulous Life* (New York: Zondervan, 2014).

Her message is simple and powerful: hard things will happen, but how you respond can change everything.[37]

Bethany's story proves that struggle doesn't have to break you. In fact, it can build you to be stronger, wiser, and more determined than ever. Embrace the struggle. Let it shape you, not stop you.

---

[37] Bethany Hamilton, "Bethany Hamilton Speaks: Overcoming Obstacles," motivational talk, accessed August 20, 2025, https:// bethanyhamilton.com.

18

Use Acute Pain to Diffuse the Constant Pain

WE ALL have those lingering sources of discomfort, the ones that quietly drain us day after day. It might be tension in a relationship, dissatisfaction at work, or just the weight of something unresolved. What we don't always realize is that short-term discomfort can be the key to long-term peace.

Choosing to face a tough moment—such as having a hard talk, quitting a job that's draining you, or admitting something difficult—can feel painful. But that momentary pain? It often frees us from much deeper, lasting hurt. In this way, leaning into acute pain becomes an act of strength and healing.

How to Implement This in Your Life

- **Spot the real struggle.** Identify what's weighing on you day to day. Where are you feeling stuck, resentful, or drained?

- **Pinpoint the hard step you're avoiding.** What action could release that pressure, even if it feels hard or scary right now?
- **Take the leap.** Whether it's starting the conversation, setting a boundary, or making a big decision, move toward the discomfort. That's where the freedom is.
- **Lean on your tools.** Deep breaths, journaling, and support from friends help you stay grounded when doing something hard.
- **Check in with yourself often.** Keep track of what you've faced, how it felt, and what changed. This builds confidence for future challenges.
- **Get comfortable being uncomfortable.** Growth and healing almost always come with some discomfort. The key is knowing it's worth it.

Real-World Example

Back in 1991, Magic Johnson made headlines for something far more personal than a game. At the height of his NBA career, he announced he was HIV positive and stepping away from basketball.[38]

In that moment, the world held its breath. The stigma around HIV was huge, and the fear was real. Magic could have kept it private. He could have avoided the questions, the headlines, and the pain, but he chose a different path.

---

[38] Lloyd, Jonathan. "Nov. 7, 1991: Magic Johnson's HIV Announcement." NBC News, November 8, 2017. https://www.nbclosangeles.com/news/local/magic-johnson-hiv-announcement/2105289/.

He chose courage. He chose truth. Yes, it hurt. That press conference brought intense scrutiny. It also opened the door to a life lived in freedom, not fear.

By confronting the acute pain of public disclosure, Magic released the constant pain of secrecy. In doing so, he changed the conversation around HIV forever. He became a symbol of strength, awareness, and resilience.

Since then, he's built a thriving life as an entrepreneur, advocate, and community leader. He's not just surviving, but thriving. It all started with one brave decision to face the pain, rather than live in its shadow.

Magic's story reminds us: sometimes the hardest steps lead to the greatest freedom. Don't be afraid to face the moment, as it could be the breakthrough you've been waiting for.

19

A Lie Is Usually Seen, Rarely Heard

IT'S EASY to say the right thing. However, if someone's actions don't match their words, that's when the truth starts to show. The phrase, "A lie is usually seen, rarely heard," reminds us to pay close attention to what people *do*, not just what they *say*.

Whether it's in your relationships, your workplace, or everyday conversations, it's often the subtle signs (like inconsistencies, body language, or behavior patterns) that reveal whether someone is being honest or not. Trust isn't built on promises. It's built on follow-through.

This mindset not only sharpens your ability to spot dishonesty but also strengthens your own integrity. When you show up consistently, speak truthfully, and align your actions with your words, people notice and trust grows.

How to Implement This in Your Life

- **Watch more than you listen.** Pay attention to people's tone, body language, and behavior. Are they congruent with what's being said?
- **Look for patterns.** A one-time slip can happen. But repeated inconsistencies? That's a red flag.
- **Walk your talk.** Want to be trusted? Let your actions prove your words. Be the example of the honesty you seek in others.
- **Check yourself.** Practice self-awareness. Are your actions giving off the message you intend? If not, take time to realign.
- **Be curious, not naive.** Question things when they don't feel right. Ask for clarification. It's not about being paranoid, but about being wise.
- **Trust your gut.** If something feels off, don't ignore it. Your instincts pick up on things your mind might not see right away.
- **Practice honest communication.** Be open and clear with people. Transparency builds relationships that last.

Real-World Example

Lance Armstrong was once one of the most admired athletes in the world. He beat cancer, won seven Tour de France titles, and built a reputation as a relentless competitor and inspiring survivor. Nonetheless, behind the scenes, another story was unfolding.

For years, Armstrong strongly denied any involvement with performance-enhancing drugs. He gave interviews, launched lawsuits, and publicly attacked anyone who questioned his integrity. On the surface, his words were convincing. Over time, the cracks started to show. This was not through what he said, but through how he acted.

Former teammates spoke out. Lawsuits piled up. His aggressive efforts to silence critics only raised more suspicion. Something didn't add up. Despite his confident denials, the behavior around him painted a different picture.[39]

In 2013, Armstrong finally admitted the truth in a televised interview with Oprah Winfrey: he had used banned substances throughout his career.[40] The fallout was massive. He lost his titles, his sponsors, and much of the public's trust. In time, Armstrong began to open up about his story—offering a more honest account, reflecting on his choices, showing personal growth, and trying to move forward.[41]

His story reminds us that actions will reveal the truth, even if words try to hide it. Integrity isn't about sounding good, it's about being good (especially when no one's watching). So watch closely. The truth is often in what you see, not what you hear.

---

[39] Juliet Macur, *Cycle of Lies: The Fall of Lance Armstrong* (New York: HarperCollins, 2014).

[40] Oprah Winfrey, *Oprah and Lance Armstrong: The Worldwide Exclusive*, OWN, January 17, 2013.

[41] Macur, *Cycle of Lies*.

20

"Everything You Want Is on the Other Side of Fear" (Jack Canfield)

FEAR HAS a sneaky way of convincing us to stay small, play it safe, and avoid risks. If you take a closer look at the moments where you've grown the most or achieved something meaningful, they almost always began with fear. This phrase reminds us that what we really want (growth, fulfillment, love, and success) is usually hiding behind the very thing we're scared to face.

Instead of letting fear be the wall that blocks your path, treat it as the doorway. Every step you take toward your fear brings you closer to the life you're capable of living. The trick isn't to eliminate fear, but to act in spite of it.[42]

---

[42] Jack Canfield, *The Success Principles: How to Get from Where You Are to Where You Want to Be* (New York: Mariner Books, 2005), 17.

How to Implement This in Your Life

- **Name your fear.** Get honest about what you're afraid of. Is it failure? Rejection? Change? Clarity is the first step.
- **Break it down.** Fear often grows in our heads. Break it into smaller parts. What's the worst that could happen? How likely is it, really?
- **Build a game plan.** Make a plan. Start small. Face fear in bite-sized pieces. A plan helps turn anxiety into action.
- **Shift the narrative.** Instead of saying or thinking, "I'm afraid," try "I'm excited." Nervous energy and excitement feel the same. Your mindset makes the difference.
- **Start small, win big.** Push yourself out of your comfort zone bit by bit. Each small win builds confidence for the next challenge.
- **Find your crew.** Don't do it alone. Let people cheer you on, give perspective, and remind you of your strength when you forget.
- **Adjust as you go.** If something doesn't work, tweak your approach. Fear loses power when you stay flexible and keep showing up.

Real-World Example

Long before she became a legend, Amelia Earhart was just a young woman with a wild dream and a sky full of doubt. Her ambition to fly (especially to cross the Atlantic solo) wasn't just bold, but unheard of. People questioned her ability, safety, and role as a woman in aviation. Instead of shrinking back, Amelia leaned into the fear.

She understood the risks. She knew the weather could turn, the equipment could fail, and one misstep could cost her life. Still, in 1932, Amelia climbed into her single-engine plane and flew solo across the Atlantic Ocean.[43] Every mile was a battle against fear, but she didn't let it stop her.

Amelia wasn't fearless, but she was brave. She chose courage over comfort and chased the possibility of something bigger. When she landed in Ireland after her flight, she made a statement: "Fear doesn't get to decide what we're capable of."[44]

Her story is a perfect example of what's possible when we stop letting fear be the limit. Amelia proved that beyond fear is freedom, purpose, and a life fully lived.

---

[43] Susan Butler, *East to the Dawn: The Life of Amelia Earhart* (Cambridge, MA: Da Capo Press, 1997), 289–94.

[44] Amelia Earhart, *The Fun of It* (Chicago: Academy Chicago Publishers, 2006 [1932]), 214–218.

21

Always Try Your Best

GIVE YOUR absolute best in everything. Whether that's at work, with loved ones, or in your personal goals, this builds something powerful. It nurtures confidence, sharpens resilience, and gives you the satisfaction of knowing you left it all on the table. Even if things don't turn out the way you hoped, you avoid the nagging question, "What if?" Over time, that consistent effort snowballs into stronger skills, new opportunities, and trust from others. Little by little, you grow into the person you aspire to be, strengthened by the simple practice of always showing up fully.

How to Implement This in Your Life

- **Set clear targets**. Define what "your best" looks like in different areas, such as work projects, hobbies, and personal growth. Clear goals give you direction and purpose.

- **Break it down**. If a goal feels daunting, divide it into smaller, more manageable steps. Focus on each one with full effort.
- **Remove distractions**. Create an environment that supports focus. Turn off notifications, and clear your space and mind.
- **Build a supporting routine**. Habit-friendly patterns (like dedicated practice time, regular exercise, or daily reflection) help you consistently bring your best forward.
- **Reflect and celebrate**. Pause regularly to look back at your progress. Acknowledge your wins (even small ones) and tune into areas for deeper growth.
- **Reframe setbacks**. When things don't go perfectly, don't judge yourself harshly. Frame it as feedback, not failure, and adjust your course.
- **Make it a habit**. Let trying your best become second nature. Do it repeatedly, even when it's not convenient. This consistency builds true character.

Real-World Example

Ever hear the story of Michael Jordan not making the varsity team as a sophomore? Well, here's the short version. In 1978, at Emsley A. Laney High School, Jordan was one of dozens competing for just a few varsity slots. It wasn't just about skill, as most sophomores didn't make varsity. As fate would have it, Jordan ended up on the junior varsity team, where he became its standout player. The next year, having trained hard and grown taller, he finally earned his place on the varsity squad.[45]

This was more than just about being good enough. Jordan's real fire was lit when he was overlooked. He later shared that seeing his friend Leroy Smith, also a sophomore, make the team while he didn't, pushed him to dig deeper.[46] That moment didn't break him. In fact, it fueled his relentless pursuit of excellence.

From that point on, Jordan refused to leave anything to chance. His legendary work ethic (and his refusal to accept "good enough") became the backbone of six NBA championships, five MVP awards, and a legacy built on unwavering effort.[47]

---

[45] Roland Lazenby, *Michael Jordan: The Life* (New York: Little, Brown and Company, 2014), 57–59.

[46] Sam Smith, *The Jordan Rules: The Inside Story of a Turbulent Season with Michael Jordan and the Chicago Bulls* (New York: Simon & Schuster, 1992), 14.

[47] "Michael Jordan Biography," *Encyclopaedia Britannica*, updated January 2024, https://www.britannica.com/biography/Michael-Jordan.

22

Find Your Peak Time and Tackle Your Most Important Tasks Then

WE ALL have that window during the day when we're at our sharpest. Our brain is focused, creative juices are flowing, and work actually feels effortless. If you can pinpoint that sweet spot and reserve it for your highest-impact tasks, you'll get more done with less stress, beat procrastination, and feel accomplished early. Over time, this simple switch can lead to better results, less burnout, and more breathing room for the rest of your life.

How to Implement This in Your Life

- **Observe your energy**. Keep tabs on when you feel most energized and productive. Track when you work best with minimal effort or distraction.
- **Test it out**. Try doing demanding tasks at different times (early morning, afternoon, evening) to discover when you thrive most.

- **Look for patterns**. Review your notes or journal entries. Identify the time window where your focus and efficiency are strongest.
- **Lock in your prime slot**. Block that high-energy window in your calendar as sacred focus time. Let everything else (like emails, calls, and small favors) fit around it.
- **Set up for success**. During your prime time, eliminate interruptions (silence notifications, prep a healthy snack, batch emails) and consider productivity tools like the Pomodoro method (breaking work into twenty-five-minute intervals separated by five-minute breaks).
- **Stay adaptable**. Energy patterns shift. Check in periodically and adjust your schedule to stay aligned with your natural rhythms.

Real-World Example

Benjamin Franklin is a legendary example of someone who understood his internal clock and used it brilliantly. He woke up at 5:00 a.m. and spent the early hours on tasks that demanded clarity and calm: planning his day, writing, studying, or tackling meaningful work with fresh energy.[48]

His routine wasn't complicated. He split his day into clear blocks: early morning for "powerful goodness" and planning, followed by four solid hours of work, a reflective afternoon, an evening of winding down, and a consistent bedtime at

---

[48] Benjamin Franklin, *The Autobiography of Benjamin Franklin*, ed. Leonard W. Labaree (New Haven: Yale University Press, 1964), 149.

10:00 p.m.[49] This rhythm helped him cover a wide range of achievements, from inventions to civic projects, by aligning his most important work with his peak mental hours.

Franklin's approach shows us that doing our best work isn't about squeezing more time into a day, but about making the most of the time we already have. Find your rhythm, guard your peak hours, and watch what you can create.

---

[49] Ibid., 150.

23

Fear Has a Voice but Not a Vote

FEAR WILL always try to speak up, whether it's a quiet worry or a loud what-if. That's natural. However, just because fear has a voice doesn't mean it gets to decide. It's on you to listen but not hand over control. By acknowledging fear without giving it the final say, you open the door to bravery, growth, and the life you want.

How to Implement This in Your Life

- **Name your fears.** Jot down what's honestly holding you back. Putting it into words can take some of its power away.
- **Listen, don't absorb.** When fear shows up, notice it, but don't assume it's telling the truth. Don't believe every thought that pops up.
- **Separate fear from reality.** Pause and assess: is this fear grounded, or just an echo from old stories? Let reason guide the decision.

- **Talk back to fear.** For fears that don't hold up under scrutiny, challenge them with questions like, "What's the worst that could realistically happen?" and, "How could I handle that?"
- **Reframe the story.** View fear as a signpost toward growth. What usually lies on the other side of fear? Something worth pursuing.
- **Take tiny steps.** You don't need to leap. A gentle step forward still moves you ahead and keeps fear from hijacking your progress.
- **Share the load.** Tell a trusted friend or mentor about your fears. Sometimes a fresh perspective helps reduce the fear.
- **Be kind to yourself.** Fear isn't a flaw, but a signal. Treat yourself with compassion when it arises.

Real-World Example

In the early 1960s, Malcolm X stood at the forefront of civil rights activism. He was a bold voice in a dangerous time. His work earned him admiration. Unfortunately, his work also earned him threats and dark warnings that made staying silent an option many would have chosen.

Before one public event in New York, Malcolm received a direct, threatening phone call: his life could be in danger if he appeared. Most people would have canceled, but not him. He listened, weighed the threat, and still chose to go on stage. Purpose, not fear, took the lead.[50]

---

[50] Manning Marable, *Malcolm X: A Life of Reinvention* (New York: Penguin Books, 2011), 287–289.

He said plainly that he feared no man, only the moral force guiding him. His reflections on fear centered on how much more his mission mattered.[51] His courage was a refusal to let fear own the outcome.

Malcolm X's life reminds us that fear might shout, but it can't cast the deciding vote. When your purpose speaks louder, you become unstoppable.

---

[51] Malcolm X and Alex Haley, *The Autobiography of Malcolm X: As Told to Alex Haley* (New York: Ballantine Books, 1964), 212.

24

Think Win-Win

THINKING "WIN-WIN" isn't about playing nice. It's about being smart and kind. Shifting from a "win-lose" mindset to one grounded in collaboration opens the door to solutions that benefit everyone. Whether you're navigating negotiations, teamwork, or friendship, it's not about outsmarting the other person. It's about co-creating success together.

How to Implement This in Your Life

- **Flip the script.** When you catch yourself viewing situations as competitions, remind yourself that there's enough success for everyone.
- **Find common ground.** In any conflict or decision, seek out shared goals or values. Questions like, "What matters most to both of us?" help guide you.
- **Communicate with heart.** Listen to understand, not to argue. Speak clearly about what matters to

you, and show you're also rooting for what matters to them.

- **Uncover what's really driving the issue.** Move past stuck positions. Clarify the deeper needs or values beneath the surface.
- **Think bigger.** Look for creative solutions where both sides gain something meaningful. Brainstorm options and leave room for innovation.
- **Celebrate together.** When collaboration leads to win-win outcomes, acknowledge it! Gratitude and positive reinforcement make future cooperation more likely.
- **Lead by example.** Show that mutual success isn't rare, but powerful. Encourage those around you to join the win-win way.

Real-World Example

When Selena Gomez launched Rare Beauty in 2020, she could have chosen a typical celebrity makeup route: sell, profit, move on. Instead, she leaned into a win-win approach: build a successful business and make a real impact.

Rare Beauty donates 1 percent of all sales to the Rare Impact Fund, a mental health initiative that aims to mobilize up to $100 million to support youth mental health programs.[52] More recently, the fund has mobilized over $20 million, sup-

---

[52] "Our Mission," *Rare Beauty*, accessed August 20, 2025, https://rarebeauty.com/pages/rare-impact.

porting thirty nonprofit organizations worldwide and reaching millions of young people.[53]

This was the foundation of her brand, not philanthropy tacked on at the end. Her customers get high-quality, inclusive beauty products. Communities gain access to mental health resources. Rare Beauty gets to grow, with purpose baked in.

Selena's work demonstrates exactly what "think win-win" looks like: building a thriving business that lifts others along the way. That's a powerful impact and a reminder that real wins don't come at someone else's expense.

---

[53] Kirsten Chuba. "Jimmy Kimmel to Host Selena Gomez's Third Annual Rare Impact Fund Benefit." *The Hollywood Reporter*, September 10, 2025. https://www.hollywoodreporter.com/lifestyle/lifestyle-news/jimmy-kimmel-selena-gomez-rare-impact-fund-benefit-1236365492/.

25

We Sink to the Level of Our Systems

MOTIVATION AND talent are powerful, but they're not always reliable. What truly sustains success are the habits, routines, and systems that carry us through the tough days. When your life is built around sturdy structures (like a morning ritual, an organized workspace, or a clear task-planning system), you don't have to rely solely on willpower. Consistency with systems brings calm, steady progress and helps you grow in the long term (even when motivation wavers).

How to Implement This in Your Life

- **Take stock of your systems.** Look at your daily life, such as your habits, environment, routines, and relationships. Which ones are helping you move forward? Which are dragging you down?
- **Watch the patterns.** Notice how different setups affect your productivity. Do distractions creep in

when your desk is cluttered or you skip your morning routine?

- **Clarify your goals.** Be crystal clear about what you're aiming for, personally or professionally. Build systems that gently support those goals.
- **Design your space for success.** Make it easy to do the right things. A clean workspace, having healthy snacks ready, and support from friends help shape successful behavior.
- **Anchor good habits.** Create routines. Whether it's a nightly reflection, regular exercise, or planning your next day, create routines that nudge you toward your goals.
- **Learn from others.** Peek at how people you admire structure their success, and then adapt their principles to fit your life.
- **Communicate openly.** If you're creating systems with others, keep the dialogue open. Ask questions like, "What's working?" "What's not?" and "What could be better?"
- **Embrace feedback.** Build quick feedback loops to fine-tune your systems so they evolve with you.
- **Collaborate for better systems.** Team up with individuals who bring different strengths. This can help amplify how your systems help everyone.
- **Stay adaptable.** What works today might not work tomorrow. Be flexible and tweak systems as your needs and circumstances evolve.
- **Reflect periodically.** Set aside time to revisit how your systems are performing. Are they still serving you? What needs a refresh?
- **Foster a growth culture.** In your own life or work, encourage a mindset of continual improvement. This is a life where systems evolve, not decay.

Real-World Example

Before Marie Kondo became a household name, she was just a passionate consultant helping people find peace in their cluttered homes. She noticed a troubling pattern: people would tidy up and feel amazing only for a moment. They would then revert to chaos. This would happen because they lacked a system, not motivation.

From that insight, Marie created what we now know as the KonMari Method. This is a repeatable system not dependent on willpower: tackle clutter by category, keep only items that "spark joy," and assign each item a home of its own. This method was about building sustainability into everyday life.[54]

When *The Life-Changing Magic of Tidying Up* hit bookshelves and later Netflix released *Tidying Up with Marie Kondo*, people were transformed by a system that stuck.[55] Their spaces stayed tidy, and mental clarity followed. Through her system, Marie showed that when our systems are strong, we live cleaner, clearer lives over time.

Her success (seen in the joy and peace her method brought to millions) is a powerful testament to the idea that our progress hinges on the strength of the systems we rely on daily.

---

[54] Marie Kondo, *The Life-Changing Magic of Tidying Up: The Japanese Art of Decluttering and Organizing* (New York: Ten Speed Press, 2014).
[55] *Tidying Up with Marie Kondo*, Netflix, 2019.

26

"Great Opportunities Never Have 'Great Opportunity' in the Subject Line" (Scott Belsky)[56]

THINK ABOUT it: the most transformative opportunities rarely come packaged in gold foil. Instead, they often arrive as ordinary tasks, unexpected challenges, or moments most people would pass up. If you wait for something obviously labeled "The Big Break," you'll likely miss the real ones hiding in plain sight. Sometimes, that unglamorous project, that chance encounter, or that "side hustle" is exactly what unlocks a breakthrough.

---

[56] Scott Belsky, *Making Ideas Happen: Overcoming the Obstacles Between Vision and Reality* (New York: Portfolio, 2010).

How to Implement This in Your Life

- **Stay curious.** Don't dismiss something just because it doesn't look flashy. Approach new ideas with genuine interest, because you never know where they might lead.
- **Ignore the hype.** Be cautious of opportunities wrapped in buzzwords and fanfare. Dig deeper to uncover substance beneath the noise.
- **Ask smart questions.** Resist the urge to jump in immediately. Instead, clarify details, ask about potential upsides or downsides, and learn the why behind the opportunity.
- **Do your homework.** Go beyond the surface. Research the context, the people involved, and past patterns. Context often reveals the real value.
- **Get a second opinion.** Bounce ideas off someone you trust. A mentor, colleague, or friend can offer perspective you might miss.
- **Test the waters first.** Rather than rushing headlong, test your opportunity in a small way. Piloting minimizes risk while revealing true potential.
- **Be patient and persistent.** Rare chances often develop slowly. Keep exploring, stay open, and don't be discouraged if something doesn't click immediately.
- **Adopt an abundance mindset.** Believe that meaningful opportunities abound even if they don't come wrapped in a bow. With that outlook, every possibility becomes fertile ground.

Real-World Example

Early in Manny Pacquiao's career, the road to superstardom was anything but clear. Having fought only in the Philippines and remaining little known internationally, he took a gamble in 2001: a last-minute call to face IBF super bantamweight champion Lehlohonolo Ledwaba.[57] It was a risky matchup, as Pacquiao was relatively unheralded, underweight, and stepping into a fight with almost no time to prepare.

On paper, it wasn't a "can't miss" opportunity. Most people saw it as a filler fight, not a game-changer. Nonetheless, Pacquiao and his team saw the hidden spark. They trained with determination and treated it as the moment to prove he belonged on the world stage.

The result? Pacquiao stopped Ledwaba in the sixth round, winning his first major world title. That unlikely victory set off a chain reaction—iconic rivalries, global fame, and a legacy as one of boxing's all-time legends.

Pacquiao's journey reminds us that sometimes the opportunities that seem the least promising are the ones with the greatest upside. They might not announce themselves with fanfare, but if you're ready to lean in, listen, and act, you'll be the one who's able to transform ordinary moments into extraordinary milestones.

---

[57] *Bobby De La Cruz.* "Looking Back at the Fight That Started It All the Pacquiao-Ledwaba Fight." Accessed June 21, 2021. https://www.boxing247.com/boxing-news/looking-back-at-the-fight-that-started-it-all-the-pacquiao-ledwaba-fight/181017.

27

"He Suffers More Than Necessary Who Suffers Before It Is Necessary" (Seneca the Younger)[58]

WORRYING ABOUT things that haven't even happened? That's a real productivity and peace killer. Seneca's timeless insight reminds us that while a little foresight can be helpful, letting anxiety about imaginary future problems take over only means we suffer twice. We suffer once in our minds now, and again if (or when) whatever we worry about actually happens. Staying grounded in today lets you conserve emotional energy, think clearly, and face actual challenges with calm confidence.

---

[58] Lucias Annaeus Seneca, *Letters from a Stoic*, trans. Robin Campbell (London: Penguin Classics, 1969).

How to Implement This in Your Life

- **Practice presence.** Whether it's meditation, a few deep breaths, or simply noticing the sights and sounds around you, tiny moments of mindfulness bring you back to now.
- **Beat catastrophic thinking.** When your mind drifts into worst-case scenarios, gently pause and ask, "Is this worry serving me today?"
- **Flip the script.** Reframe challenges as opportunities. In other words, look at challenges as chances to grow rather than things to fear.
- **Manage negative inputs.** Be intentional about your media consumption. Too much doom-scrolling fuels fear that often doesn't reflect reality.
- **Prioritize self-care.** Nourish your resilience through exercise, time outside, creative outlets, or restful sleep.
- **Lean on support.** Surround yourself with voices that remind you to stay present, not panicked. A friend, mentor, or loved one can help break the cycle of fear.
- **Plan, then step back.** If a concern is real, plan for it and then release it. There's no need to carry worry once you've taken action.
- **Cultivate gratitude:** regularly acknowledging what's good right now helps quiet what might go wrong tomorrow.

Real-World Example

A perfect case is the prolonged arms race of the Cold War. Driven by mutual suspicion and fear of falling behind, the US and the USSR poured trillions into building nuclear arsenals. This spending was based largely on what might happen, not what was happening.[59]

The result? Massive budgets diverted from infrastructure, a world living under the constant shadow of possible annihilation, and decades of psychological and economic stress. Meanwhile, both sides would have likely benefited more from diplomacy and measured restraint.

This chapter in history shows how anxiety about what could go wrong often causes far more suffering than the actual crisis would have. Seneca's wisdom held true here. The fear of future threats turned into real harm (emotional, financial, and societal), causing everyone to lose, while the imagined enemy might have been talking from the same worry-ridden place.

---

[59] John Lewis Gaddis, *The Cold War: A New History* (New York: Penguin Books, 2005).

28

Use Energy Like You Use Electricity: Intelligently

YOUR ENERGY (mental, emotional, physical) is one of your most valuable assets. Think of it like electricity: powerful, finite, and capable of lighting up everything from big ideas to meaningful connections. Feelings like anxiety, anger, or fear often bring a surge of energy. Instead of letting that go to waste or spiral out, you can channel it into real change. Just like you choose what to plug in at home, you get to choose where your energy flows in life. When you're intentional about how and where you spend your energy (like focusing on what truly matters, setting limits, and nurturing what fuels you) you create a more focused, energized, and fulfilling version of your day-to-day.

How to Implement This in Your Life

- **Track your energy usage.** Notice where your time and energy go each day. Are there people, habits, or thoughts that leave you feeling drained? Spot the leaks and start patching them up.

- **Focus on what moves the needle.** Tackle your most important goals when your energy is at its best. Just like you'd power your fridge before you'd plug in a lava lamp, make sure your core priorities come first.
- **Protect your power source.** Say "no" more often. Your energy is precious, so avoid taking on things that don't align with what really matters to you.
- **Recharge on purpose.** Rest isn't a luxury, but a requirement. Build in downtime, movement, and fun to keep your internal battery strong and steady.
- **Clean up your headspace.** Negative thoughts can suck your energy faster than a dead-end meeting. Practice mindfulness, gratitude, or journaling to stay grounded and focused.

Real-World Example

Back in the 1930s, as India was fighting for freedom from British rule, many leaders wanted to respond with violence. Mahatma Gandhi had a different approach. He knew that anger could be a powerful force, but only if directed wisely. Instead of reacting emotionally, he turned the country's frustration into focused action.

One powerful moment was the Salt March in 1930. Gandhi and thousands of followers walked 240 miles to the sea to protest British salt taxes, not with rage, but with peaceful defiance. It was a simple act, but it sent shockwaves around the world and sparked nationwide resistance.[60]

Gandhi's story is a powerful reminder: your energy can do incredible things when you use it wisely. He didn't waste it fighting everything. He funneled it into a single, clear mission. Just like electricity, it's not how much you have, but how you use it that changes everything.

---

[60] Judith M. Brown, *Gandhi: Prisoner of Hope* (New Haven: Yale University Press, 1991), 218–220.

29

Choose a Growth Mindset, Not a Fixed One

THIS IDEA is powerful because it changes how you see yourself and the world. Instead of viewing challenges and failures as proof that you're not good enough, a growth mindset helps you see them as stepping stones to learning and improvement. A growth mindset means that you believe that with effort, practice, and a willingness to learn, you can grow your skills and overcome obstacles.[61] When you embrace this mindset, you become more open to trying new things and are better able to bounce back from setbacks and push yourself further. A fixed mindset, on the other hand, can keep you stuck, afraid to fail, and resistant to change. Choosing a growth mindset opens doors to more confidence, resilience, and long-term success in every part of your life.

---

[61] Carol S. Dweck, *Mindset: The New Psychology of Success* (New York: Ballantine Books, 2006), 6–12.

How to Implement This in Your Life

- **Notice your mindset.** Start by checking in with yourself. What do you believe about your intelligence, talent, or ability to grow?[62] Notice if you ever think, "I'm just not built for this." That may be your fixed mindset talking.
- **Welcome challenges.** Try saying yes to things that stretch you. Whether it's a new project at work or learning a new skill, leaning into tough stuff helps you grow stronger.[63]
- **Talk to yourself differently.** Swap out limiting thoughts like, "I can't do this," with something more empowering, like, "I haven't mastered this yet, but I can learn." The words you use matter more than you think.
- **Aim to learn, not just win.** Set goals that focus on learning something new or getting better at something. Do this rather than just hitting numbers or beating others.
- **Ask for feedback.** Reach out to people you trust for honest, constructive feedback. Listen with an open mind and use it as fuel to grow, not as proof you're failing.
- **Celebrate progress.** Don't just wait for the big wins. Celebrate every step forward. Each bit of progress builds your confidence and keeps the momentum going.
- **Make learning a habit.** Commit to growing every day. Read books, take classes, watch tutori-

---

[62] Ibid., 13–31.
[63] Ibid., 32–58.

als, or explore something new. Keep feeding your curiosity.

- **Use setbacks as teachers.** When things don't go your way, don't shut down. Take a step back, figure out what went wrong, and use the experience to improve for next time.
- **Build a growth-minded circle.** Surround yourself with people who lift you up and believe in growing too. It's easier to stay motivated when you're in good company.
- **Be kind to yourself.** When you hit a wall, treat yourself like you would a friend. Everyone struggles sometimes. What matters most is how you respond.

Real-World Example

Long before Pedro Pascal became a breakout star in *The Mandalorian* and *The Last of Us*, he spent years hustling through small roles and near misses. Audition after audition ended in rejection, and it would've been easy to give up. A fixed mindset might have told him, "Maybe I'm just not good enough," but Pedro chose to keep going.

He sharpened his craft in theater, took minor roles on TV, and treated every failure as a lesson.[64] He's shared in interviews how he stayed curious and kept improving, even when things felt discouraging.

---

[64] Karen Valby. "Everyone Wants a Piece of Pedro Pascal." *Vanity Fair*, June 2025. https://www.vanityfair.com/ hollywood/story/ pedro-pascal-cover-story?srsltid =AfmBOoo_Tz3CmleALsgOZQBH3 PGxC Y0b6a 7fRuGQezxg 2WqO Mu5MS3J0.

Then in 2014, his role as Oberyn Martell on *Game of Thrones* finally put him on the map.[5] From there, bigger roles followed, but they came after years of persistence and a belief that his skills could grow.

Pedro's journey is a great reminder: success doesn't come from never failing, but from learning, growing, and showing up again and again with a mindset that says, "I'm not done yet."

30

If a Dog Bites You Once, It's the Dog's Fault. If a Dog Bites You Twice, It's Your Fault

THIS SIMPLE metaphor reminds us that the first time someone hurts you—through bad deals, betrayal, or misguided trust—it can be chalked up to circumstance. However, if the same mistake happens again and you didn't adjust your approach, that's on you. These moments are calls to sharpen your boundaries, wise up your judgment, and hold yourself accountable so you steer toward healthier relationships and opportunities in the future.

How to Implement This in Your Life

- **Reflect on the lesson.** When something fails or someone lets you down, pause to understand what went wrong and treat the event as an important clue.

- **Set a guardrail.** If something or someone has caused harm before, don't go in blind again. Ask questions, draw boundaries, or change course entirely.
- **Notice patterns.** If you see the same red flags showing up, don't just brush past them. Instead, honor what's happening and recalibrate.
- **Own your role.** When a repeat scenario unfolds, ask yourself: "What could I have done differently?" That question is where real change starts.
- **Be smart, not paranoid.** This isn't about closing yourself off. It's about engaging with more awareness and clarity.

Real-World Example

Early in Dwayne "The Rock" Johnson's wrestling career, things did not go smoothly. His first WWE persona, Rocky Maivia, was supposed to be a heroic character that fans would rally behind. Instead, the crowd turned on him. They booed him, chanted, "Die, Rocky, Die," and rejected the very image he was trying to project. That first rejection stung. It was the first bite.[65] For many people, that level of public failure might have been enough to break their confidence. The Rock could have stayed stuck in that version of himself, repeating the same mistakes, waiting for the audience to change, but he knew better.

---

[65] Shaun Assael and Mike Mooneyham, *Sex, Lies, and Headlocks: The Real Story of Vince McMahon and the WWF* (New York: Crown, 2002), 227–230.

Instead of staying in a narrative that clearly was not working, he used it as fuel. He studied what fans responded to, paid attention to his weaknesses, and began to shift his approach. He doubled down on training so his performance in the ring spoke for itself. He widened his persona, no longer just relying on his athleticism, but building charisma that went beyond his physical presence. He started adding humor, quick wit, and a sharp edge to his character. In short, he learned from the first bite and made sure he would not be caught off guard by the second.

He also worked behind the scenes to grow. He partnered with the right agents, listened to advice, and took control of his brand.[66] The character that emerged (The Rock) was a version of himself amplified: confident and layered with personality. Fans who once booed him began to cheer. They connected with the authenticity he brought once he stopped forcing a version of himself that wasn't true.

So when Hollywood came calling, he was not simply reacting to luck or chance. He had already done the hard work of reinventing himself with intention. He stepped into acting with the same discipline he applied to wrestling, honing his craft and refusing to let the first chapter of rejection define the rest of his story. By the time opportunities arrived, he was ready to seize them fully.

The Rock's rise from early heartbreak in wrestling to global superstardom was no accident. It was the result of calculated evolution. He did not rebuild in the same place he had fallen. He learned, adapted, and chose smarter paths forward. That

---

[66] Dwayne Johnson and Joe Layden, *The Rock Says . . .* (New York: HarperCollins, 2000), 115–118.

is the essence of the lesson: the first bite may catch you by surprise, but if you let yourself get bitten the same way again, that is on you. The Rock shows us that success is not about avoiding failure altogether, but about refusing to repeat it once you see it for what it is.

31

Resistance Is Most Powerful at the Finish Line

THINK ABOUT the last time you were moments away from a big accomplishment like finishing a project, achieving a goal, or hitting a milestone. It's usually right then that doubt creeps in, distractions pile up, or fatigue sets in. That final stretch, the "finish line," is often when resistance is at its fiercest. By expecting this and staying committed, you can push through and savor the incredible growth that comes from completing what you started.

How to Implement This in Your Life

- **Spot your finish line.** Identify key projects or goals you're nearing. These are your moments to stay extra vigilant.
- **Plan for pushback.** Near the end, self-doubt, fatigue, and external pressure tend to intensify. Be proactive. Rehearse how you'll stay focused, manage fatigue, and resist distractions.

- **Celebrate small wins.** Even big goals are made of small victories. Pause along the way to acknowledge your progress. It keeps your morale strong and energy high.
- **Find your team.** Accountability and encouragement matter most when resistance hits. Lean on a trusted friend, coach, or mentor to keep you grounded and motivated when things feel heavy.

Real-World Example

When Emma Grede co-founded Good American with Khloé Kardashian, she challenged fashion norms by launching a denim line in 2016 with sizes ranging from 00 to 24, all at the same price.[67] That idea alone was groundbreaking, but the hardest battle came at the finish line.

As launch day approached, the resistance hit hard. Manufacturers doubted inclusive sizing would succeed. Retail partners hesitated to stock a brand breaking standard molds. Inside the team, last-minute production hurdles and nerves began to swirl. At that critical moment, it felt like everything could fall apart.

Emma didn't let it. She leaned into the pressure, confronted objections head-on, and kept the launch on track. The result?

---

[67] McEvoy, Jemima. "Keeping Up with the Kardashians: Meet the Woman Who Made a Fortune Helping Build the Family's Billion Dollar Business Empire." *Forbes*. June 14, 2022. https://www.forbes.com.

Good American's debut became the biggest launch in denim history, raking in $1 million on day one.[68]

Emma's story shows exactly why resistance at the finish line isn't a signal to stop, but a sign you're close to something big. Push through, and you might just break records.

---

[68] Ibid.

32

Always Contemplate How You Can Turn a Negative Situation into a Positive One

WHEN SOMETHING goes sideways in life, the first step (before rushing to react) is to pause and ask, "How might this situation be reshaped for good?" Even if an immediate fix feels out of reach, shifting your mindset this way changes everything. You move from feeling stuck to feeling empowered. You start to notice potential where before there was only frustration. Turning negativity toward possibilities not only builds resilience but also eases stress. Over time, this proactive approach can transform tough moments into growth, learning, and clearer pathways forward.

How to Implement This in Your Life

- **Practice mindfulness.** Take a few breaths and fully inhabit the moment. This quiet focus helps you see beyond the immediate problem and opens space to consider next steps.
- **Identify the lesson.** After facing a setback, honestly ask, "What can I learn from this?" Sometimes that lesson plants the seed for a smarter next move.
- **Shift your narrative.** Replace, "This is awful," with, "What can I do differently going forward?" Simple language shifts like this steer you toward solutions instead of spirals.
- **Brainstorm without judgment.** Jot down every idea, no matter how small or strange. Sometimes innovation starts with the oddest spark.
- **Lean on others.** Talk through challenges with supportive friends, mentors, or loved ones. Their perspective might shine light on options you hadn't imagined.
- **Build gratitude into the moment.** Even during hardship, anchor yourself by noticing small positives. This gentle shift nurtures positivity and perspective.
- **Break it down into goals.** Turn a large, overwhelming issue into small, actionable steps. Each step forward builds momentum and optimism.
- **Use affirmations.** Keep a few affirming phrases handy (like, "I can learn from this") to reset your outlook when negativity creeps in.
- **Visualize a bright outcome.** Picture how things will feel once resolved. Your mind loves a narrative. The hopeful ones help push action.

- **Reflect regularly.** Weekly or monthly, revisit past challenges. Celebrate how you navigated them, what you learned, and how you grew stronger.
- **Celebrate your efforts.** Even if the outcome isn't perfect, acknowledge the fact that you faced it and tried. Your growth is in the trying.

Real-World Example

A profound example comes from Viktor Frankl, the psychiatrist and Holocaust survivor who authored *Man's Search for Meaning*. Imprisoned in Nazi concentration camps, Frankl faced unimaginable hardship and loss. Instead of surrendering to despair, he resolved to find meaning even in suffering. He did so by supporting fellow prisoners, reflecting on human dignity, and identifying purpose amid the worst conditions.[69]

This choice, to turn suffering into a kind of teaching and connection, allowed him to survive emotionally and mentally. After the war, he developed *logotherapy*, a therapeutic approach centered on finding meaning in life, even amid suffering.[70] Logotherapy shows us that while we can't always change our circumstances, we can transform our response, making even the darkest experiences a source of growth and compassion.

Frankl's life shows that the reflection on negativity, when guided by mindfulness, meaning, and choice, builds enduring strength. It also illuminates paths forward, even in the most challenging of times.

---

[69] Viktor E. Frankl, *Man's Search for Meaning*, trans. Ilse Lasch (Boston: Beacon Press, 2006), 65–80.

[70] Frankl, *Man's Search for Meaning*, 104–115.

33

Always Have Something to Look Forward to in Life

HAVING SOMETHING to look forward to, whether big or small, adds a sense of joy and direction to life. It gives your days purpose and makes it easier to push through the tough ones. Just the anticipation of something good can lift your mood and boost your motivation. It creates a spark, helping you stay hopeful, bounce back from stress, and feel more in control of your path. When you're working toward something meaningful, you tend to plan better, stay focused, and feel more fulfilled. By building a life with regular moments of excitement, growth, and joy on the horizon, you'll keep your energy and spirit moving forward in a positive way.

How to Implement This in Your Life

- **Get clear on what excites you.** Think about what genuinely lights you up, whether it's a dream trip, learning something new, or hitting a milestone at work or in your personal life. Set goals that matter to you, and map out simple steps to get there.

- **Keep a "joy list."** Always have a few things on the calendar you're excited about: maybe a dinner with friends, a fun vacation, or a concert down the line. Refill your list often so there's always something new coming up to look forward to.

- **Celebrate the small stuff.** Don't wait for big wins to feel good. Notice and enjoy the little milestones along the way. Whether it's completing a task, getting through a hard day, or starting something new, every step is worth recognizing.

- **Try something new.** Keep life interesting by exploring new hobbies, visiting unfamiliar places, or simply mixing up your routine. New experiences keep your mind engaged and give you fresh things to be excited about.

- **Share the excitement.** Talk about what you're looking forward to with people you trust. Sharing that joy brings it to life, deepens your relationships, and helps you stay in a forward-thinking mindset.

Real-World Example

Maya Angelou (the celebrated writer, artist, and activist) lived a life full of achievement. She wrote books that changed the cultural landscape, delivered poetry that stirred hearts, and lent her voice to causes that mattered. Yet even after decades of recognition, awards, and worldwide respect, she never settled into the comfort of her past accomplishments. She always had her eye on what was next. For her, success was not a resting place, but a springboard.

In the 1990s, long after publishing *I Know Why the Caged Bird Sings* and cementing her place in literary history, she kept seeking out new ways to express herself. She stepped into directing, took on performing, and made space to mentor young creatives who were finding their own voices. She approached each new opportunity with the same sense of wonder that had guided her early career. When asked why she chose to keep exploring new paths, her answer was simple but profound: having something ahead to grow into kept her feeling alive.

Even in her role as a professor at Wake Forest University, Maya carried that same energy. She saw teaching as a shared journey. She would often tell her students how excited she was to witness their growth, but also her own. She believed that each class, each conversation, and each project was an opportunity to stretch herself in new ways. "I'm always writing, always hoping, always looking forward to the next great idea," she once said.[71] Those words were not just a reflection of her career, but of her spirit.

Maya's life offers a powerful reminder. No matter where we find ourselves on our journey, there is always more to anticipate. There is always another chance to grow, to learn, to create, and to stretch beyond what we thought possible. That forward-looking spirit is what keeps us energized, curious, and fully alive. Her example shows us that it is not about clinging to what we have already done, but about embracing what is still ahead.

---

[71] Maya Angelou, quoted in *Conversations with Maya Angelou*, ed. Jeffrey M. Elliot (Jackson: University Press of Mississippi, 1989), 104.

34

Regular Quiet Time Fuels Motivation

IN TODAY'S noisy world, carving out quiet time is essential. Giving yourself at least two 2-hour sessions a week without screens, noise, substances, or distractions helps you recharge mentally and emotionally. It's a reset button for your brain. When you step away from constant notifications and background noise, your mind slows down. You think more clearly, reflect more deeply, and begin to sort through your thoughts with more intention. This kind of clarity boosts motivation and focus. It helps you see your priorities more clearly, come up with creative ideas, and process emotions that might otherwise get buried. Quiet time can also help improve sleep and your overall relationship with tech. You feel more energized, less overwhelmed, and more in control of your time and mental space.

How to Implement This in Your Life

- **Put it on the calendar.** Treat quiet time like an important meeting. Choose two times during the week and block them off in your schedule. Don't let anything bump it.
- **Choose a good spot.** Find a calm, comfortable place with minimal distractions. It could be a cozy corner, your backyard, or a quiet park bench.
- **Set the vibe.** Turn off all tech, dim the lights, and maybe light a candle or open a window for some fresh air. The goal is to create a space that invites calm and reflection.
- **Use the time intentionally.** Try meditation, journaling, deep breathing, or just sitting quietly. This isn't about doing nothing. It's about creating space for your thoughts and emotions to surface.
- **Minimize temptation.** Leave your phone in another room. Shut the laptop. Let people know you're unavailable. Quiet time only works if you fully disconnect.
- **Try, tweak, repeat.** See what works best for you. Maybe two hours is too long to start. Try thirty minutes and build up. The key is consistency.
- **Sneak in quiet moments daily.** Even short pauses, like a five-minute breath break or a walk without your phone, can be powerful. Use them to stay grounded throughout your day.

___

Real-World Example

Tim Ferriss, bestselling author and entrepreneur, swears by scheduling quiet, screen-free "thinking time." In *Tools of Titans*, he explains how stepping away from the constant pull of devices and unplugging regularly, especially in nature, has shaped some of his most important life and business decisions. He describes how easy it is to become trapped in cycles of busyness, where every moment is filled with meetings, emails, and notifications. For a while, he lived like that himself, constantly pulled in different directions and spread too thin. Eventually, the pressure built to the point where he knew something had to change.

That breaking point led him to experiment with what he now calls "deloading" days. Instead of stacking his schedule with obligations, he began setting aside intentional time to reflect, recharge, and realign with his priorities. Sometimes this looked like long walks outdoors without a phone. Other times it meant sitting quietly with a notebook, free from distractions. By carving out this space, he discovered that ideas began to surface more naturally. Problems that once felt overwhelming suddenly had solutions. What had seemed urgent often revealed itself to be unimportant, while what truly mattered rose to the top.

Ferriss has credited this practice with giving him the clarity to make smarter choices, both personally and professionally.[72] It gave him the margin to step back, notice what was working, and course-correct before burnout set in. More importantly,

___

[72] Timothy Ferriss, *Tools of Titans: The Tactics, Routines, and Habits of Billionaires, Icons, and World-Class Performers* (Boston: Houghton Mifflin Harcourt, 2016), 39–41.

it reminded him that progress does not always come from grinding harder. Sometimes, it comes from creating enough stillness to hear your own thoughts clearly.

His story is a reminder that shutting out the noise is not just an escape, but a strategy. In that quiet space, you make room for fresh insight and deeper motivation. When you return to your work, you do so with a sharper sense of direction, a lighter spirit, and a focus on what really matters.

35

Practice Gratitude: Be Grateful for the Positives in Your Life

TAKING THE time to genuinely feel grateful for the positives in your life has a profound impact. Gratitude shifts your focus from what's missing to what's already abundant. It helps ease stress and anxiety by inviting feelings of contentment and appreciation. When we acknowledge what's good (be it people, experiences, or little everyday joys), we also strengthen our relationships, improve sleep, and boost our energy. Gratitude builds self-esteem and resilience, making us better equipped to handle challenges. In the long run, this simple practice nurtures a more optimistic, hopeful, and fulfilled approach to life.

How to Implement This in Your Life

- **Keep a gratitude journal.** Every day, jot down a few things you're thankful for. These can be big moments, kind gestures, or everyday comforts.

Reflecting on them can shift your mood and mind-set in powerful ways.

- **Thank the people around you.** Tell someone what you appreciate about them, such as a friend's encouragement, a co-worker's help, or family support. These small expressions of gratitude deepen bonds and foster kindness.
- **Pause and notice.** In your day-to-day, pause to savor what's good: the warmth of sunlight, a favorite song, or someone's smile. Noticing these moments helps reinforce a grateful mindset.
- **Surround yourself with reminders.** Use visual cues (like a note board, gratitude jar, or simple quote) to gently prompt you to practice appreciation throughout your day.
- **Find the gift in challenges.** When trouble strikes, take a moment to identify what you can be grateful for, perhaps a lesson learned or a hidden strength. Reframing difficulty with gratitude builds resilience.

Real-World Example

Helen Keller, deaf and blind from early childhood, may have faced overwhelming adversity, but she championed gratitude as a cornerstone of her life. What could have been a story only of limitation became instead a story of appreciation, resilience, and purpose. She learned early on that gratitude was not dependent on perfect circumstances. Rather, it was something she could carry within her. It was a way of noticing the good that was present even when much had been taken away.

Her teaching and support team, especially Anne Sullivan, became a source of deep appreciation. Anne's patience and persistence opened the world to Keller in ways that once seemed impossible. Through Anne's guidance, Keller came to recognize how much even small victories mattered. Each breakthrough in communication and each new concept grasped was celebrated with thankfulness. That gratitude did not stay private. She expressed it openly, letting those around her know how much their support meant. In doing so, she reinforced the bonds that carried her forward.

Keller also learned to value life's simple pleasures. She frequently expressed thankfulness for things that others might overlook, such as the warmth of sunlight on her skin, the scent of flowers drifting through the air, or the gentle touch of a friend's hand.[73] These experiences became anchors, reminders that beauty and joy could still be found even in the absence of sight and sound. Her gratitude for these moments was not superficial. It was an active practice that shaped her ability to endure hardship without losing hope.

Despite the immense challenges she faced, Keller dedicated her life to helping others. She wrote, lectured, and advocated for people with disabilities, always carrying with her a profound sense of appreciation for the opportunities she had been given.[74] Her gratitude became fuel for her mission, allowing her to see beyond her struggles and focus on lifting others up.

---

[73] Helen Keller, *The Story of My Life* (New York: Doubleday, Page & Company, 1903), 132–135.

[74] Dorothy Herrmann, *Helen Keller: A Life* (Chicago: University of Chicago Press, 1999), 214–218.

Her life stands as a powerful reminder that gratitude is not a passive feeling, but a deliberate choice. Even in the darkest circumstances, it can spark resilience, meaning, and joy. Keller shows us that when we choose to notice and appreciate the good, no matter how small, we unlock the strength to keep moving forward and to help others do the same.

36

Find the Fire That Motivates You

WHEN YOU discover what truly lights you up inside (your personal "fire"), you tap into what matters most to you: your passions, your values, and the things that give your life meaning. That kind of inner motivation lasts longer and runs deeper than chasing money, titles, or approval. Once you know what fuels your drive, you can point your energy in the right direction, toward projects and goals that actually mean something to you. That kind of clarity can supercharge your focus, help you push through challenges, and make your hard work feel more fulfilling.

How to Implement This in Your Life

- **Give yourself time to reflect.** Find quiet moments to journal, meditate, or simply think about what truly excites and inspires you. What makes you feel fully alive? What values do you hold close?

- **Notice what you're good at and what you love.** Make a list of your natural strengths and the topics or activities you could talk about or do for hours. Your true passions usually live right where your talent and enthusiasm meet.
- **Try new things.** Say yes to classes, hobbies, or experiences outside your usual routine. Sometimes you don't find your fire, but instead stumble into it by being open to new possibilities.
- **Ask people who know you well.** Friends, family, or mentors often see gifts in us that we overlook. Ask them what they think makes you special or where they've seen you shine.
- **Align your actions with your spark.** Once you get a feel for what motivates you, start adjusting your goals and routines to reflect it. Be flexible. It's okay if your passions shift or grow over time.
- **Celebrate the little wins.** Every step forward matters. Give yourself credit for progress, even if it feels small. That validation helps keep your spark burning.
- **Learn from people who inspire you.** Look into how others, like Oprah Winfrey, discovered and followed their passions. What steps did they take? What obstacles did they face and overcome?

Real-World Example

In the early days of her career, Mindy Kaling was hustling on every front. She was interning wherever she could, squeezing in stand-up sets at small venues, showing up to auditions, and writing on the side late into the night. The grind was constant, and the rejections piled up. She kept hearing "no," often not because of a lack of talent, but because she did not fit Hollywood's usual mold. Casting directors looked for a certain type, and she was told, over and over again, that she was not it. For many people, that kind of feedback could have been enough to make them quit. Mindy refused to let those rejections define her path.

Instead of waiting endlessly for someone else to give her a chance, she decided to create her own. She leaned into what excited her, what made her laugh, and what she wanted to see on stage. With that energy, she co-created a satirical play, *Matt & Ben* (2002), which flipped the script by reimagining the origin story of Matt Damon and Ben Affleck. She and her writing partner performed it themselves, putting their voices and creativity out into the world without waiting for permission. It was a bold move. It was not a guaranteed success, but it allowed her to showcase her wit and originality in ways no audition room ever had.

The risk paid off. Audiences and critics noticed the sharp humor and unique perspective she brought, and suddenly the industry began to see what she had known all along. They could see that her voice mattered. That project cracked open the door to bigger opportunities, leading to her landing her first major role as both writer and actor on *The Office* (2005–2013).[75] On that show, she didn't just contribute jokes; she became an essential creative force, writing some of the series' most memorable episodes while bringing a fresh and relatable character to life on screen.

---

[75] Mindy Kaling, *Is Everyone Hanging Out without Me? (And Other Concerns)* (New York: Crown Publishing, 2011).

Mindy's journey shows that waiting for someone else to choose you can be a trap. She didn't just stumble into her fire; she recognized it and pursued it wholeheartedly. She followed what gave her energy, and in doing so, she built her own platform rather than waiting for one to appear. Her story is a reminder that when you stop waiting to be picked and instead invest in the work that lights you up, incredible things can happen. Your fire not only motivates you, but it can change everything about the direction of your life.

37

Life's Greatest Opportunities Run on Their Own Schedule

WE OFTEN expect opportunities to follow our plans, but life doesn't work like that. We must stay open and ready, even when things don't happen when we want them to. Instead of sticking rigidly to our timelines, this mindset invites us to stay curious and flexible. You begin to notice possibilities that once seemed insignificant and avoid frustration when the timing isn't perfect. Embracing this view helps build resilience and adaptability. So when life's big moments arrive (often unexpectedly), you're ready to meet them with intention and confidence.

How to Implement This in Your Life

- **Practice patience and presence.** If you're frustrated by delays or missed opportunities, take a breath. Remind yourself that things often unfold when they're supposed to, not when we demand. Focus on the now, not the someday.

- **Reframe setbacks.** When a plan falls through or you hit a roadblock, ask, "Could this delay actually be setting the stage for something better?" Let curiosity replace disappointment.
- **Trust the process.** Know you're doing what you can and let life do the rest. Avoid micromanaging outcomes. Life often opens the right doors when you lean into your purpose.
- **Notice the subtle signs.** Stay alert to small cues or synchronicities that might guide you to new directions. Opportunity often arrives quietly.
- **Celebrate the little wins.** Even small breakthroughs matter. They're often the breadcrumbs leading to larger paths. Acknowledging them keeps optimism alive.
- **Find role models.** Look to people like Vincent van Gogh, whose major recognition came posthumously. His story reminds us that success doesn't always follow conventional timelines and can surprise us.
- **Journal your journey.** Write down what you notice about timing, patience, and life's unfolding. Over time, you'll see patterns and gain deeper insight into how your own opportunities emerge.

Real-World Example

Vera Wang is now a global fashion icon. However, her career did not start out that way. What makes her story remarkable is that her journey did not begin in design at all. As a young woman, her dream was to compete as a figure skater. For years she trained with the goal of making the 1968 US

Olympic team. She poured her energy into the rink, chasing that vision with discipline and determination. When she did not make the team, the path she had imagined for herself ended abruptly. For many, that kind of disappointment might have lingered, keeping them tied to a dream that no longer fit. Wang chose to pivot instead. She redirected her ambition into a completely different world: fashion.

Her entry into that industry was not a small step. She secured a role at *Vogue*, where she worked her way up through dedication and an eye for style that stood out. Over the course of seventeen years, she proved herself again and again until she became the magazine's youngest-ever senior editor.[76] That role gave her influence and experience, but eventually she moved on to Ralph Lauren, continuing to stretch her skills and see the industry from new angles. She was willing to leave behind comfort in order to grow.

Then came another turning point, one that would change not only her career but the entire bridal industry. At age forty, an age when many feel it is too late to reinvent themselves, Wang decided to experiment with bridal fashion. She noticed a gap in the market, a lack of modern, stylish gowns that reflected the individuality of brides. In 1990, she launched her first bridal gown collection. The risk was enormous, but the results were undeniable. Her designs redefined what bridal wear could look like—elegant yet innovative, classic yet fresh. Brides around the world suddenly had an alternative to traditional gowns, and her work reshaped the industry.

---

[76] Biography.com Editors, "Vera Wang," *Biography*, last modified April 2, 2014, https://www.biography.com/fashion-designer/vera-wang.

That debut did more than introduce her as a designer. It launched a career that would grow into one of the most iconic names in fashion, a brand recognized and respected worldwide. It happened years after her initial ambitions as an athlete had shifted. Her path was not linear, and it did not follow a predictable timeline. Nonetheless, each pivot added to the foundation that allowed her to succeed when the moment was right.

Wang's story shows that the path to opportunity rarely unfolds in a straight line. Instead, it is built on flexibility, resilience, and a willingness to trust your evolving journey. Her greatest breakthrough came not when she clung to her first dream, but when she allowed herself to grow beyond it. That decision at forty became the turning point that changed everything. This serves as a reminder that it is never too late to reinvent yourself and seize the chance that may not have existed in your original plan.

38

Epiphanies Happen Either When You Switch Off or by the Dissent of Others

EVER NOTICE how your best ideas hit you in the shower, on a walk, or during a moment of calm? That's no coincidence. True "aha!" moments often show up when we finally give our minds a break or when someone challenges how we think. "Switching off" allows your subconscious to connect dots you didn't even know were related. Likewise, hearing a dissenting opinion can shake us out of our mental rut and offer a new, valuable perspective. Both stillness and outside input can be uncomfortable, but they open doors to deeper insight, creativity, and growth. When you lean into both, you set yourself up for moments of clarity that can shift everything.

How to Implement This in Your Life

- **Unplug regularly.** Set aside dedicated time each week to disconnect from devices, notifications, and distractions. Whether it's a digital detox day or a quiet evening walk, these breaks create the space where new ideas can spark.

- **Meditate or get outside.** Meditation, breathwork, or a peaceful hike can help you quiet the mental noise. These moments of stillness help you tune into inner wisdom and surface insights you didn't know were waiting.

- **Invite contrasting opinions.** Make it a habit to read, watch, or listen to ideas that challenge yours. Talk to people from different walks of life. Let their perspectives expand your own, even if it's uncomfortable at first.

- **Be curious, not defensive.** When someone questions your thinking, pause before reacting. Listen with the intention to understand, not to respond. Often, buried inside that disagreement is a breakthrough.

- **Journal your insights.** Write down reflections, conversations that shifted your thinking, and random sparks of inspiration. Over time, these entries become a goldmine of wisdom and perspective.

- **Keep an "idea bank."** Create a space (a notebook, app, or vision board) to stash ideas that come to you, no matter how rough or half-baked. Review it regularly. You'll be amazed at what develops with time.

- **Stay humble and flexible.** No one knows it all. Stay open to being wrong or learning something new. Growth often begins with the words, "I hadn't thought of it that way."

Real-World Example

Justice Ruth Bader Ginsburg didn't just revolutionize gender equality; she also embraced both quiet reflection and the power of opposing viewpoints.

Early in her legal career, Ginsburg was often overlooked and underestimated. Instead of giving in to frustration, she used that quiet time to think deeply about injustice and how to tackle it. These quiet moments shaped her vision for changing the law.[77]

She didn't stop at internal reflection. She also actively sought out feedback, even the uncomfortable kind. For example, before arguing *Frontiero v. Richardson* (1973), a colleague gave her some tough criticism about her legal brief. Instead of brushing it off, she listened, reworked her strategy, and came back stronger.[78] That case became a major win for women's rights.

Throughout her life, Ginsburg combined deep inner clarity with an openness to being challenged. That's part of what made her such a force for change.[79] Her story shows that when we give ourselves space to think and the courage to listen to others, we create the perfect environment for life-changing epiphanies.

---

[77] Mary Hartnett and Wendy W. Williams, *Ruth Bader Ginsburg: A Life* (New York: Simon & Schuster, 2018), 87–89.

[78] Irin Carmon and Shana Knizhnik, *Notorious RBG: The Life and Times of Ruth Bader Ginsburg* (New York: Dey Street Books, 2015), 102–105.

[79] Jeffrey Rosen, *Conversations with RBG: Ruth Bader Ginsburg on Life, Love, Liberty, and Law* (New York: Henry Holt and Co., 2019), 45–47.

39

"What You Seek Is Seeking You" (Rumi)[80]

WHEN YOU have a clear intention or goal, the universe, or your own subconscious mind, conspires to bring opportunities and experiences aligned with that intention into your life. By aligning your actions and thoughts with your desires, you will increase the likelihood of encountering opportunities that support your goals. This encourages a proactive approach, understanding that actively seeking something makes one more receptive to finding it. This occurs through a change in perspective or the emergence of new possibilities.

How to Implement This in Your Life

- **Be present.** Ground yourself in the here and now through meditation, deep breathing, or even simple "pause" breaks. Presence sharpens your awareness of the signs and synchronicities waiting to connect.

---

[80] Jalāl al-Dīn Rūmī, *The Essential Rumi*, trans. Coleman Barks (San Francisco: HarperCollins, 1995), 106.

- **Trust your gut.** Let intuition guide you alongside logic. Pay attention to those subtle nudges, as your instincts are often smarter than you think.
- **Clarify your desires.** Spend quiet time journaling or contemplating what really matters to you, beyond titles or trends. True clarity attracts the right energy.
- **Stay open to surprises.** Expect magic in the mundane. That unexpected message, chance meeting, or new idea could be the universe whispering your way forward.
- **Let go of the reins.** Release the urge to micro-manage every detail. When you let go of how it should happen, the magic often shows up in ways you never expected.
- **Celebrate the mini-wins.** Notice every step forward, even the small ones. Each one signals movement toward what you're aligning with.
- **Surround yourself with inspiration.** Engage with stories, people, and communities that embody this principle.

Real-World Example

Howard Schultz, the former CEO of Starbucks, is a great example of how, "What you seek is seeking you," can play out in real life. Growing up in a working-class neighborhood in Brooklyn, Schultz dreamed of building something meaningful and lasting. While working at Starbucks in its early days (when it only sold coffee beans), he traveled to Italy and was inspired by the coffee bar culture he experienced there: the community, the ritual, the connection.[81]

He pitched this idea to Starbucks' leadership, but they weren't interested. Instead of giving up, Schultz decided to leave Starbucks and open his own coffee bar, Il Giornale, based on what he saw in Italy. It was a hit. Years later, Starbucks was struggling, and he had the chance to purchase Starbucks and bring his original vision to life.[82] Schultz bought Starbucks and helped to build it into the coffee shops that you visit today.

Schultz's journey shows that when you're passionate and willing to follow that spark (even when others don't see it yet), opportunities find their way to you. His dream of creating a welcoming, community-centered coffee shop wasn't just his own desire, but something the world was quietly waiting for too.

---

[81] Howard Schultz and Joanne Gordon, *Onward: How Starbucks Fought for Its Life without Losing Its Soul* (New York: Rodale, 2011), 19–25.

[82] Howard Schultz and Dori Jones Yang, *Pour Your Heart Into It: How Starbucks Built a Company One Cup at a Time* (New York: Hyperion, 1997), 41–52.

40

You Have to Be Good Every Day to Be Great

THE TRUTH? Greatness isn't the result of one big leap. It's the sum of thousands of tiny, consistent steps. When you show up every day by training your mind, refining your skills, being effective, and being kind, you build a foundation that success can stand upon. By aiming to be "good" consistently (not perfect), you open the door to lasting achievement and a life marked by steady growth.

How to Implement This in Your Life

- **Set daily targets.** Choose simple, doable goals each morning. Finish a task, learn a phrase, or send a thoughtful message. Your small actions add up.
- **Build a routine.** A rhythm that balances work, self-care, and reflection turns small actions into habits.
- **Stay mindful.** Practice presence. Breathe, focus, and let your attention serve your daily efforts. Avoid distractions.

- **Lean on self-discipline.** Make keeping your word to yourself a priority, especially on days when motivation is low.
- **Reflect nightly.** At day's end, check in on what went well and what you'd tweak. Self-awareness fuels progress.
- **Ask for insight.** Feedback (even small phrases like "great pace" or "more clarity, please") gives you direction for change.
- **Never stop learning.** Feed your curiosity daily. Read, listen, and practice. Small growth compounds.
- **Celebrate tiny wins.** Whether you made someone smile or learned something new, acknowledge it. It nurtures your mindset.
- **Stay adaptable.** Not every day will go perfectly. When life slows you down, adjust your efforts.
- **Fill your circle with positivity.** Surround yourself with people who model and cheer on consistent effort. It makes the habit easier to keep.

Real-World Example

Take Roger Federer. He's often called the GOAT (greatest of all time) in tennis. But before that, he was a kid with big talent and even bigger work ethic. Every single day, Federer refined his mindset, honed his fitness, sharpened his technique, and embraced discipline.

Over a two-decade pro career, Federer didn't rest on early wins. He practiced strategically, recovered wisely, and competed with a quiet intensity. And even as injuries and younger competitors emerged, he stayed on his path. He was focused, deliberate, and consistently improving.[83]

His journey wasn't about one epic match. It was about choosing excellence daily by training, adapting, and staying grounded. That mindset brought him Grand Slams and global respect. It shows us that greatness isn't built overnight. It's earned incrementally, one purposeful day at a time.[84]

---

[83] Christopher Clarey, *The Master: The Brilliant Career of Roger Federer* (New York: Twelve, 2021), 112–115.

[84] Christopher Clarey, *The Master: The Brilliant Career of Roger Federer* (New York: Twelve, 2021), 342–345.

41

If You're Not Going Forward, Then You're Going Backward

LIFE DOESN'T wait for us. If we're not growing, we're actually falling behind. This principle is a reminder to guard against complacency and keep moving forward. Environments shift, skills get outdated, and opportunities pass by. Maintaining the status quo is illusory. It's only through actively pursuing growth and improvement that we really progress. Embracing this mindset encourages regular self-reflection, helps you spot where you're stuck, and pushes you to adapt. Over time, consistency in forward momentum breeds fulfillment and success.

How to Implement This in Your Life

- **Check in with yourself regularly.** Set a monthly or quarterly "growth audit." Ask, "Am I learning something new? Pushing past comfort? Making progress toward what matters?

- **Spot what's stalling.** Identify areas (emotional, mental, physical, professional) where you're feeling stuck. Choose one and make a plan for moving forward again.
- **Define inspiring goals.** Create targets that pull you into the future, both short-term or longer-term. Make sure they're specific, meaningful, measurable, and aligned with your values.
- **Never stop learning.** Feed your curiosity, whether through books, workshops, or hands-on exploration. Learning is never wasted. Everything adds forward momentum.
- **Experiment boldly.** Try new routines, ideas, or habits even if they feel uncomfortable. Treat them as experiments. Every attempt sharpens your path.
- **Surround yourself with growth-minded people.** Find friends, mentors, or communities that push you forward. Their energy and stories can spark ideas and keep you accountable.
- **Celebrate micro-wins.** When you progress, even in small ways, acknowledge it. Those tiny boosts keep motivation alive and prevent slipping into stagnation.

Real-World Example

Look at how Ryan Reynolds moves through life. After the massive success of *Deadpool* in 2016, most would've played it safe by taking similar roles and riding out the fame. Reynolds chose to keep moving.

In 2018, he invested in Aviation Gin not just as an investor, but as a creative force. He jumped into marketing and scripted ads that blended his wit with compelling branding. That bold move turned Aviation Gin into a serious contender, eventually leading to a $610 million acquisition by Diageo in 2020.

Reynolds didn't stop there. He co-founded Maximum Effort, a marketing and production company. He also co-acquired Wrexham AFC with Rob McElhenney in 2020.[85] Through smart storytelling and community engagement, they turned the football club into a global sensation.[86] In addition, Reynolds continues to seek out and be a part of new ventures.

Ryan Reynolds's journey shows why moving forward (even when things are going well) matters. You might lose ground if you stand still. He didn't just stay in motion doing the same things. He expanded his reach, built new ventures, and redefined his influence well beyond his acting career.

---

[85] Smith, Rory. "Welcome to Wrexham: It's the Future." *New York Times*, September 19, 2022.
[86] Ibid.

42

In Order to Be a Level 10 Person, You Must Be at a Level 10 in Personal Development

THIS IDEA is simple but powerful. To truly excel in any area of life, you first have to grow within. That means building self-awareness, strengthening your emotional intelligence, and always seeking ways to better yourself. Why? Because your outer success (whether it's in your career, relationships, or creativity) is capped by how strong you are on the inside. When you commit to personal development, you build the skills and mindset to go the distance. You're more equipped to handle tough moments, spot new chances, and stay focused on what matters most. Personal growth is essential if you want to show up as your best self and perform at the highest level in every part of life.

How to Implement This in Your Life

- **Check in with yourself regularly.** Every few months, take time to assess where you are in key areas of your life, such as your health, mindset, emotional well-being, learning, and integrity. Rate yourself honestly on a scale of 1–10, and pinpoint where you want to grow.
- **Build a plan that fits your life.** Create a personalized roadmap for growth. Include small goals, daily habits, and ways to track progress. Make sure your plan touches all parts of you. Focus on your body, heart, mind, and spirit.
- **Get to know yourself deeply.** Use journaling, meditation, therapy, or feedback from others to uncover how you think, what you feel, and where you can grow. Self-awareness is the foundation of real progress.
- **Learn from people you admire.** Find mentors, teachers, or inspiring figures who live at a high level. Ask for advice, join a group, or study their stories. Their wisdom can guide and fast-track your journey.
- **Never stop learning.** Keep feeding your curiosity. Take courses, read books, attend events, or teach yourself new skills. Every bit of learning is a step toward becoming the next best version of you.
- **Surround yourself with growth-minded people.** Spend time with friends, colleagues, and communities that uplift and challenge you. Being around people who care about self-improvement keeps you inspired and accountable.
- **Celebrate your progress.** Recognize the small wins along the way. Whether it's finishing a book, build-

ing a habit, or handling a tough situation better than before, every step forward deserves a little celebration.

Real-World Example

Tony Robbins didn't start with an easy path. Growing up in a financially unstable and often chaotic home, he could have let his environment define him. Instead, he decided early on that he wanted to grow and help others do the same. As a young man, Tony dove headfirst into personal development, learning from greats like Jim Rohn and constantly applying what he learned.[87]

Even while building his career as a speaker and coach, Tony kept sharpening his skills, attending workshops, reading constantly, and pushing his own limits. He ran dozens of seminars a year and kept evolving as a leader, all while helping millions transform their lives.[88] His event, Unleash the Power Within, has inspired countless people to face their fears and pursue their dreams.

Tony's journey proves that if you want to reach level 10 in life, you have to work on yourself first. His commitment to growth not only led to his own success, but it also gave others permission to chase theirs. He's a living example of what's possible when you make personal development a daily habit.

---

[87] Tony Robbins, *Unlimited Power: The New Science of Personal Achievement* (New York: Free Press, 1986).

[88] Tony Robbins, *Awaken the Giant Within: How to Take Immediate Control of Your Mental, Emotional, Physical, and Financial Destiny!* (New York: Simon & Schuster, 1991).

43

Find a Mentor

HAVING A mentor in your corner can be one of the most rewarding experiences in your personal and professional journey. A great mentor offers more than just advice. They also give you fresh insights, honest feedback, and encouragement when you need it most. They help you see things from different angles, point out blind spots, and push you to grow. Mentors often open doors to networks and opportunities that would be tough to reach on your own. They speed up your learning curve, helping you avoid mistakes and make smarter decisions. Just as important, they inspire confidence, help you stay grounded during tough times, and remind you of your potential. A solid mentor-mentee relationship is about forming a supportive bond that fuels long-term growth and purpose.

How to Implement This in Your Life

- **Reflect on your growth areas.** Start by asking yourself, "Where could I use some extra guidance or wisdom?" Maybe it's a new skill you're trying to master, a career leap you're aiming for, or a big life change on the horizon.

- **Identify potential mentors.** Think about people who've walked a path you admire. Do some research, ask around, or follow individuals who have the kind of experience or qualities you'd like to learn from.
- **Establish clear expectations.** When you connect with a potential mentor, be honest about what you're looking for, what you hope to gain, and how much time you can both commit. Clarity up front helps the relationship thrive.
- **Cultivate the relationship.** Be present, curious, and open to learning. Listen more than you speak, ask meaningful questions, and show appreciation for your mentor's time and input.
- **Be proactive and accountable.** Take responsibility for your growth. Come to meetings prepared, follow through on feedback, and stay committed to applying what you learn.
- **Offer value in return.** Find ways to give back. Maybe it's helping with a project, sharing a useful connection, or simply being a sounding board. Mentorship is a two-way street.
- **If you can't find the right mentor, don't let that stop you.** The internet is packed with stories, interviews, and lessons from people who've done what you aspire to do. Study their paths and let their experiences guide you forward.

Real-World Example

When Mark Zuckerberg was building Facebook into a global company, he found himself at a crossroads. The platform was growing at a rapid pace, attracting millions of new users and transforming the way people connected online. However, with that growth came major decisions about the company's direction, culture, and long-term vision. At that stage, Zuckerberg knew he needed perspective from someone who had already navigated the difficult terrain of building a world-shaping company. So he reached out to Steve Jobs for guidance.

Jobs encouraged him to think beyond numbers and market share. He challenged Zuckerberg to go deeper and to root everything in Facebook's mission and purpose.[89] For Jobs, the true measure of success was in whether it stayed aligned with its core reason for existing. That perspective helped Zuckerberg reframe the challenges he was facing, reminding him that clarity of purpose would be the compass through seasons of rapid change.

Zuckerberg later shared that one of their most impactful conversations took place during a walk at Apple's campus. Jobs did not deliver a lecture filled with metrics or technical advice. Instead, he spoke about the importance of building with heart and intention. He explained that great companies are sustained by the spirit behind the work. This includes the values, passion, and sense of meaning that inform every deci-

---

[89] Walter Isaacson, *Steve Jobs* (New York: Simon & Schuster, 2011), 553–554.

sion.[90] Hearing this from someone who had already walked that path left a lasting impression.

That message stuck with Zuckerberg and influenced how he led Facebook through moments of uncertainty. This included difficult product decisions and questions about growth. He began to see that leadership was about continually returning to the *why* behind the mission. That reminder gave him clarity during times when the way forward seemed unclear.

Their relationship is a perfect example of how the right mentor can do more than offer practical tips or quick fixes. A mentor can help you zoom out, connect with your deeper purpose, and approach challenges with a renewed sense of confidence. Jobs's guidance gave him the conviction to lead with clarity, heart, and intention.

44

When Engaging with Others, Always Give a Compliment or Say Something Positive

MAKING A habit of giving someone a genuine compliment or saying anything positive may seem like a small act, but it works wonders in building stronger connections. A heartfelt compliment not only makes someone's day, but also sets the tone for positive interaction. It shows you see the best in them, which fosters mutual respect, trust, and goodwill. In tense situations, a sincere kind word can act like a soothing balm, making conversations smoother and more constructive. Whether at work or home, thoughtful praise supports collaboration, deepens bonds, and brings out the best in relationships for the giver and the receiver.

How to Implement This in Your Life

- **Do this daily.** Tell yourself: "I'll share something kind today," whether with a co-worker, a neighbor, or even yourself.
- **Be specific.** Instead of generic praise, highlight something real, like the way someone stayed calm in a crisis or how you admire their persistence.
- **Make it personal.** Tailor the compliment to the individual. Show you notice and appreciate what makes them unique.
- **Match your body to your words.** Smile, make eye contact, and choose an encouraging tone. Your warmth speaks volumes.
- **Mind the moment.** Tact matters. Sometimes it's best to compliment quietly; other times, publicly letting someone know they're appreciated makes a big impact.
- **Listen first.** When someone shares their wins, listen with curiosity. Your genuine response shows you're truly engaged.

Real-World Example

The story of Fred Rogers, the beloved host of the children's television series *Mister Rogers' Neighborhood*, is a powerful example of how this simple yet profound practice can have a transformative impact.

Throughout his long career as an educator, minister, and television personality, Fred Rogers was renowned for his ability to make each child he interacted with feel special, valued, and worthy of love and respect. This was evident in the way he engaged with his young viewers, offering them sincere, heartfelt compliments and affirmations.

Rather than simply lecturing or preaching, Rogers had a gift for connecting with children on a deep, emotional level. He often paused to acknowledge their feelings, validate their experiences, and highlight their unique strengths and talents. His genuine, positive interactions left a lasting impression on generations of young people.[91]

But Rogers's commitment to positivity extended far beyond his work on television. In his personal life, he made a habit of seeking out opportunities to offer genuine compliments and encouragement to the people he encountered, whether it was a colleague, neighbor, or complete stranger.[92]

This practice of "always giving a compliment or saying something positive" was rooted in Rogers's deeply held belief in the inherent worth and dignity of every human being. He understood that a few kind words could have the power to uplift someone's spirit, boost their confidence, and inspire them to reach their full potential.

Rogers's story is a testament to the transformative impact that can occur when we make a conscious effort to infuse our interactions with genuine positivity. By consistently offering sincere compliments and affirmations, he not only bright-

---

[91] Maxwell King, *The Good Neighbor: The Life and Work of Fred Rogers* (New York: Abrams Press, 2018), 145–147.
[92] Amy Hollingsworth, *The Simple Faith of Mister Rogers* (Nashville: Thomas Nelson, 2005), 62–64.

ened the lives of those around him, but also cultivated a legacy of empathy, compassion, and the belief in the goodness of humanity.

45

Trust Your Gut

WE TALK a lot about logic, strategy, and planning in life. But there's another decision-making tool people overlook because it feels "mystical." It isn't. It's your intuition. It's your gut. Learning to trust it can change the entire trajectory of your life.

Your gut isn't some random emotional impulse. It's the part of you that has been silently collecting data your entire life. Your subconscious has stored every mistake, every win, every heartbreak, and every moment you've ever paid attention to without realizing it. And sometimes it recognizes patterns long before your logical mind can catch up. That's why a situation can "feel off" before you can explain why.

Trusting your gut means listening to that internal signal instead of drowning it out with overthinking, fear, or other people's expectations. When something feels wrong, it usually is. When something feels aligned (when your body relaxes, your energy lifts, or you feel an unexplainable pull) that's your intuition nudging you toward the right direction.

The more you trust your gut, the more confidence you build in your own judgment. And that confidence compounds. It becomes self-belief. It becomes momentum. It becomes wisdom.

How to Implement This in Your Life

- **Pay attention to your first reaction.** Your initial feeling often reveals your most honest truth before fear or overthinking has a chance to interfere. Notice the immediate sense of ease or discomfort that surfaces when making a decision.
- **Listen to your body's signals.** Your intuition often speaks through physical cues like tension, calmness, or a sudden shift in energy. Treat these sensations as valuable information rather than dismissing them.
- **Create quiet moments to hear yourself.** Intuition is easier to access when your mind isn't crowded. Give yourself space to breathe, reflect, and let your inner voice rise above the noise of daily life.
- **Reflect on past choices.** Look back at moments when trusting your gut led you in the right direction—or when ignoring it created problems. These reflections strengthen your ability to recognize your intuition in real time.
- **Let intuition guide you while logic supports you.** Your gut can point you toward the direction that feels most aligned, and your reasoning can help you take thoughtful, strategic steps forward. Both can work together.
- **Pay attention to what feels forced.** When you repeatedly have to convince yourself to move

forward, it's usually a sign your gut is saying no. Decisions that feel natural and aligned often point to a clearer yes.

- **Act on clear intuitive signals.** When something feels undeniably right or undeniably wrong, trust that feeling and take action. The more you follow your intuition, the more confident and self-assured you become.

Real-World Example

Simone Biles, one of the most decorated gymnasts in history, is an inspiring example of what it looks like to trust your gut. From a young age, she pushed herself to new heights, mastering routines no one else had attempted. Her path was not an easy one. She faced overwhelming pressure, personal struggles, and intense public scrutiny. What set her apart was her self-confidence, consistency, discipline, and the way she gave her all every day.

In a defining moment at the 2021 Tokyo Olympics, Simone knew she was not in the right mental space to compete and made the brave decision to step back from competition to prioritize her mental health.[93] Although it did not appear so to some, that choice was the ultimate act of self-respect and wisdom. Simone reminded the world that trying your best sometimes means trusting your gut and making an unpopu-

---

[93] D'Arcy Maine. "Simone Biles Withdraws from Individual All-Around Gymnastics Competition at Tokyo Olympics to Focus on Mental Well-Being." *ESPN.* July 28, 2021. https://www.espn.com/olympics/gymnastics/story/_/id/31902290/simone-biles-withdraws-individual-all-competition-tokyo-olympics-focus-mental-health.

lar decision. Fully healed and mentally prepared to give her best effort, Simone returned for the 2024 Olympics and won three gold medals and one silver medal for her performances. Her journey is proof that greatness isn't about being perfect; it's about showing up, doing the work, and staying true to yourself. Her story challenges us to meet our own lives with the same heart, drive, and honesty.

46

Seize the Moment

EVER NOTICE how the most unforgettable experiences happen when you step in, not step back? When you choose to act decisively on an opportunity instead of hesitating, you open the door to growth, excitement, and meaningful progress. Saying "yes" to the moment fuels adaptability and resilience. It teaches you to roll with what life brings, instead of waiting for a perfect scenario. When you seize the moment, you spend less energy on regret, and more on living. You build courage, foster spontaneity, and remind yourself that you're the one steering the ship.

How to Implement This in Your Life

- **Stay present.** Whether you're in traffic or enjoying a quiet moment, stay aware of what's happening around you. Mindfulness gives you the window to spot opportunities you'd otherwise miss.
- **Say yes sometimes.** Invite spontaneity. Skip the plan and try something new, such as a walk, a

unique sport, or a surprise event. You never know when that "yes" turns into a life-changing moment.

- **Trust your inner voice.** When your gut nudges you toward something bold like an idea, a person, or an adventure, lean in. Of course, do it wisely, but don't ignore your instincts.
- **Go for what matters.** Fill your schedule with people, activities, and experiences that feel meaningful, not just filler.
- **Skip paralysis by analysis.** If you're stuck choosing or waiting for certainty, let your desires guide you. Action (speaking your truth, picking a path) beats passivity.

Real-World Example

Richard Branson, the famous founder of the Virgin Group, is a living, breathing example of what it means to truly "seize the moment." His story is packed with bold moves, quick thinking, and a fearless attitude that's helped him build an empire by saying "yes" when others might hesitate.

Branson's entrepreneurial spark started early. At just sixteen, he launched *Student* magazine.[94] From there, his ventures grew wildly across industries, all under the Virgin name. What really sets him apart is how he jumps on opportunities, even when they come out of the blue.

---

[94] Richard Branson, *Losing My Virginity: How I Survived, Had Fun, and Made a Fortune Doing Business My Way* (New York: Crown Business, 1998), 35–40.

Take one classic Branson moment in the 1970s. He was stuck at an airport after his flight got canceled. Most people would've just waited it out, but not Branson. He rented a plane and sold the extra seats to other stranded passengers, and just like that, the idea for Virgin Atlantic was born.[95] One canceled flight turned into a multi-billion-dollar airline.

That's how he operates. He is always alert and always ready. He's not afraid to step into the unknown, trust his gut, and chase after what excites him. His career is proof that great things can come from spontaneous decisions and that fortune often favors the bold.

What's inspiring about Branson is that he doesn't just talk about grabbing life by the horns, he lives it. His energy is contagious, and his story encourages others to stop over-thinking and start acting. He shows us that sometimes, the door doesn't open until you give it a push.

So if there's one thing Branson's journey teaches us, it's this: don't wait. Be curious. Take the risk. Embrace the moment. That's often where the magic begins.

---

[95] Richard Branson, *Finding My Virginity: The New Autobiography* (New York: Portfolio/Penguin, 2017), 145–147.

47

Have Empathy and Give People Grace: Everyone Is Going Through Something

LET'S BE real, we all navigate unseen battles. That's why empathy and grace aren't just nice-to-haves, but are essential for real connection. When we show up with genuine understanding, even when someone stumbles, we reduce conflict and deepen trust. Instead of judgment, empathy invites patience and kindness. Grace gives others room to mess up and learn. It softens harsh interactions and builds stronger, more supportive relationships. In nurturing empathy for others and ourselves, we help shape a kinder, more emotionally intelligent world, one interaction at a time.

How to Implement This in Your Life

- **Really listen.** When you're talking with someone, pause your inner response and truly absorb what they're saying. Ask questions. Reflect back key points. Let them know you hear them, because you do.
- **Hit pause on judging.** Before drawing conclusions about someone's actions, remember that you don't know their full story. That pause builds empathy.
- **Grant grace first.** If someone's words sting or their actions fall short, lean toward understanding instead of assuming the worst. Often, kindness shifts everything.
- **Speak with care.** Words can hurt or heal. Aim for compassion. Approach conversations looking for solutions, not to assign blame.
- **See the world through others' eyes.** Seek out stories or conversations with people whose experiences differ from your own. It'll expand your compassion in ways you never expected.
- **Remember your own challenges.** Recall a time when someone cut you slack or showed you kindness when you needed it. Let that guide how you respond now.
- **Celebrate small acts of kindness.** When you see someone show empathy or grace, shine a light on it. Thank them or quietly acknowledge their compassion. Your recognition can inspire more of it.

Real-World Example

In 1999, while filming *The Matrix*, Keanu Reeves was already one of the most recognizable stars in Hollywood. Behind the scenes, his life was marked by profound personal loss. Only a year earlier, his longtime girlfriend, Jennifer Syme, had given birth to their daughter, who was stillborn.[96] The grief of that tragedy weighed heavily on both of them, and not long after, Syme was killed in a car accident.[97] For most people, carrying that level of heartbreak would make it hard to show up with kindness, but Keanu never allowed his pain to turn into bitterness toward others.

Throughout his career, he has been known for his empathy in small, human moments. On the subway, he has been photographed giving up his seat for strangers. On set, crew members share stories about how he treats them with the same respect he shows his co-stars. One widely shared story came from the filming of *The Matrix Reloaded*, when he learned that several crew members were struggling financially. Quietly, without seeking attention, he gave away millions of dollars from his own earnings to support the special effects and stunt teams, insisting that their work was just as vital as his own.

These acts were not about image or publicity. They were rooted in his deep understanding that everyone is carrying unseen struggles. Keanu, having endured so much himself, chose to meet people with empathy and grace. He gave gen-

---

[96] Dan Hall. "Inside Matrix star Keanu Reeves' tragic life after girlfriend's freak death and baby heartbreak – before he found love." *The Sun*, December 22, 2021. https://www.the-sun.com/entertainment/4321803/keanu-reeves-matrix-resurrections-tragic-life/.

[97] Ibid.

erously, listened openly, and never made others feel small in his presence.

His life reminds us of the truth behind the phrase: "Have empathy and give people grace. Everyone is going through something." We may not always see another person's battles, but kindness costs us nothing, and it can make all the difference.

48

Learn How to Motivate Others

LEARNING TO motivate others can completely transform your relationships and the way you work with people. It brings out the best in those around you, builds trust, and helps everyone move forward together. Whether you're at work trying to boost team morale or at home encouraging a loved one, motivation deepens connection and brings out shared purpose. It starts with really understanding what makes someone tick (like their hopes, challenges, and what lights them up). From there, you can connect with them in a way that feels real and supportive. Being able to inspire others also makes you a better leader and a more reliable friend or partner. It's about creating a positive, encouraging environment where people feel seen, appreciated, and excited to grow.

How to Implement This in Your Life

- **Get curious about what drives people.** Spend time really listening to the people around you. What do they care about? What excites or worries them? The more you understand their personal motivations, the better you'll be at lifting them up.

- **Celebrate the small wins.** A kind word or simple acknowledgment can go a long way. Be specific and heartfelt when you recognize someone's effort. It helps them feel proud and keeps their momentum going.

- **Challenge people in a supportive way.** Give others tasks that stretch them just enough to grow. Help them see the challenge as a chance to prove something to themselves, and let them know you believe in them.

- **Encourage a growth-oriented outlook.** Remind people that they don't have to be perfect. Frame mistakes as learning opportunities and show that progress matters more than perfection.

- **Lead with compassion.** Sometimes people need more than motivation. They need someone who gets what they're going through. Be that person. Offer support without judgment.

- **Paint the bigger picture.** Help others understand how their efforts fit into something larger. Whether it's a team goal or a shared dream, showing the impact of their work can reignite motivation.

- **Let people take the lead.** Give them space to figure things out on their own. Offering trust and flexibility shows respect and gives people room to take ownership and feel proud of their contributions.

- **Walk your talk.** The most powerful motivation often comes from example. When others see you showing up, pushing forward, and staying positive, they'll feel inspired to do the same.

Real-World Example

DJ Khaled became not just a music producer, but a self-made motivational guru. This was especially true on Snapchat, where he delivered daily doses of encouragement through his now-iconic "Keys to Success." His frequent phrases like, "They don't want you to win," and, "Major key alert," weren't just catchy, but were intentional motivators for millions. By persistently reinforcing positivity, self-belief, and resilience in an upbeat and authentic way, Khaled inspired people to stay focused and uplifted in their own journeys.[98]

What made his approach so powerful? It stemmed from truly understanding his audience. He spoke directly, played to the emotions of hope and hustle, and used his Snapchat platform to rally people toward their best selves. His motivational style created a tightly connected community that thrived on encouragement, optimism, and the belief that success is within reach.[99]

By mastering how to motivate others through daily, relatable messages, DJ Khaled turned social media into a stage for empowerment.[100]

---

[98] Sam Lansky. "How DJ Khaled Became the Self-Help Sage of Snapchat." *Time.* May 5, 2016. https://time.com/4319116/dj-khaled-snapchat/.
[99] Ibid.
[100] Ibid.

49

Progress Every Day

LIVING BY this idea means showing up for yourself consistently, one step at a time. It's not about huge leaps, but about making enough progress each day to move closer to your goals. This approach builds momentum and helps you feel accomplished, even on tough days. By focusing on the little wins instead of obsessing over the end result, you stay motivated and engaged. You begin to see growth as something continuous, not sudden. Over time, those small efforts really add up. This also builds self-discipline, helping you stay consistent with your actions. When you make daily progress, you feel better about yourself and more confident in your abilities. This mindset encourages a positive, proactive outlook and leads to long-term success and fulfillment, both personally and professionally.

How to Implement This in Your Life

- **Create clear, doable goals.** Break your big dreams into smaller, more achievable steps. Focus on what you can do today that will move you forward, even if just a little.

- **Build a daily habit that supports you.** Find a daily practice that aligns with your goals (like journaling, exercise, or skill-building) and make it a non-negotiable part of your routine.
- **Keep track of what you're doing.** Use a notebook, app, or spreadsheet to log your progress. Even the smallest accomplishments matter, and seeing them add up will keep you inspired.
- **Celebrate your wins.** When you hit a milestone or complete a goal for the day, take time to recognize it. These small celebrations fuel long-term motivation.
- **Learn something new every day.** Set aside a little time each day to grow. Whether that's reading, listening to a podcast, or trying something new, continuous learning keeps your progress fresh and exciting.

Real-World Example

Gilbert Arenas's journey from an overlooked high school athlete to one of the NBA's most electrifying scorers is a powerful reminder of what it means to embrace "progress every day."

Growing up under tough circumstances in Los Angeles, Arenas faced real obstacles (both personal and financial) that could've easily knocked him off course.[101] Instead of giving

---

[101] Fred Barnes. "Gilbert Arenas: The Assassin." *washingtonian.com.* November 1, 2006. https://www.washingtonian.com/2006/11/01/gilbert-arenas-the-assassin/.

in, he locked in. From a young age, he committed to getting better day by day, putting in the work to fine-tune everything from his jump shot, to his defense, to his conditioning.

Even when the season ended, his drive didn't. While others rested, Arenas kept pushing. Oftentimes he trained multiple times a day. He treated each day as another chance to level up. That relentless hustle helped him earn a scholarship to the University of Arizona, where teammates and coaches quickly noticed that his dedication was just as strong as his talent.

In 2001, Arenas was drafted thirty-first overall by the Golden State Warriors. He was a pick that many didn't expect much from. However, he proved the doubters wrong. Through consistent, focused effort, he climbed the ranks and became a three-time NBA All-Star known for putting up huge scoring numbers and clutch performances.

When a serious knee injury threatened to end his career, Arenas once again leaned on his "progress every day" mindset. His rehab was slow and painful, but he stayed committed, rebuilding his strength and returning to compete at a high level once more. Gilbert continues to progress every day. He recently started a sports podcast that quickly became very popular.

Gilbert Arenas's story shows us that success is about steady, daily effort. By focusing on improving just a little every day, he went from overlooked to unstoppable. His path is a reminder that when you show up consistently, even the biggest goals can become possible.

50

Be Proactive

TAKING INITIATIVE isn't just about doing things early. It's about taking charge of your life rather than letting it control you. Being proactive gives you confidence, reduces stress, and significantly boosts your chances of success. You begin to anticipate obstacles, and instead of reacting in panic, you've already thought through solutions. That foresight sharpens your problem-solving skills and helps you seize opportunities before they slip away. You build resilience as you learn to navigate challenges on your own terms. In short, being proactive transforms your entire approach to life, grounding you in agency, confidence, and purpose.

How to Implement This in Your Life

- **Scan for what's next.** Keep an eye on what's ahead. Watch for challenges and possibilities in your work and relationships. Start crafting solutions before issues appear.

- **Set actionable goals.** Write down clear, measurable goals and break them into bite-sized steps. Daily action plans help you move forward intentionally.
- **Keep learning ahead of time.** Don't wait until you're stuck to grow. Proactively build skills that prepare you for what might come next.
- **Build your crew.** Surround yourself with people who support your proactive spirit, like mentors, collaborators, and thinkers who challenge and propel you.
- **Try new things experimentally.** Take calculated risks and learn from failures. Growth happens when you step outside the familiar.
- **Step out of reaction mode.** Notice when you're reacting, procrastinating, scrambling, or waiting for others. Then shift. Choose your next move instead of waiting for it.
- **Speak up early.** In conversations or meetings, voice concerns and ideas before they become problems. Bring solutions, not just issues.
- **Celebrate your moves.** Every step counts, even the ones that don't immediately pay off. Reward yourself for the proactive effort; it keeps the momentum alive.

Real-World Example

Bad Bunny's journey from being a regular kid in a small Puerto Rican town to becoming one of the biggest global music stars is a masterclass in being proactive. He didn't wait around for someone to discover him. He took matters into his own hands, putting his music online and building a connection with fans one song at a time.[102]

In those early days, he worked a grocery store job during the day and made music deep into the night. He created his own sound by blending different styles and staying true to himself. He turned social media into his stage, treating every post like a performance, using it to grow his fanbase and refine his identity as an artist.

Even after he made it big, Bad Bunny never got comfortable. He kept moving forward, collaborating with unexpected artists, experimenting with fresh sounds, and speaking out on topics that mattered to him. Everything he did was with purpose, showing that being proactive is about constantly evolving and steering your future.

His story is proof that when you take initiative instead of waiting for approval, you can carve out your own lane in life.

---

[102] Ben Beaumont-Thomas, "How Did Bad Bunny Become the World's Biggest Pop Star?" *The Guardian*, December 4, 2020. https://www.theguardian.com/music/2020/dec/04/how-did-bad-bunny-become-the-worlds-biggest-pop-star.

The Wise AF Principles

1. The Golden Rule: treat others as you would want to be treated.
2. How you do one thing is how you do everything.
3. "Observation without evaluation is the highest form of human intelligence" (Jiddu Krishnamurti).
4. "Hard choices, easy life. Easy choices, hard life" (Jerzy Gregorek).
5. "Movement is life" (Aristotle).
6. Control what you can control.
7. Wake up early.
8. Put first things first.
9. Time kills deals.
10. Listen to your body.
11. Be a problem solver.
12. If one way does not work, what are you doing differently?
13. "First seek to understand, then to be understood" (Stephen R. Covey).
14. Everything in moderation.
15. Spend time with friends and/or family at least once per week.
16. Catch up on current events at least once per week.
17. Embrace the struggle.
18. Use acute pain to diffuse the constant pain.
19. A lie is usually seen, rarely heard.
20. Everything you want is on the other side of fear.
21. Always try your best.

22. Find your peak time and tackle your most important tasks then.
23. Fear has a voice but not a vote.
24. Think win-win.
25. We sink to the level of our systems.
26. "Great opportunities never have 'great opportunity' in the subject line" (Scott Belsky).
27. "He suffers more than necessary who suffers before it is necessary" (Seneca the Younger).
28. Use energy like you use electricity: intelligently.
29. Choose a growth mindset, not a fixed one.
30. If a dog bites you once, it's the dog's fault. If a dog bites you twice, it's your fault.
31. Resistance is most powerful at the finish line.
32. Always contemplate how you can turn a negative situation into a positive one.
33. Always have something to look forward to in life.
34. Regular quiet time fuels motivation.
35. Practice gratitude: be grateful for the positives in your life.
36. Find the fire that motivates you.
37. Life's greatest opportunities run on their own schedule.
38. Epiphanies happen either when you switch off or by the dissent of others.
39. "What you seek is seeking you." (Rumi)
40. You have to be good every day to be great.
41. If you're not going forward, then you're going backward.
42. In order to be a level 10 person, you must be at a level 10 in personal development.
43. Find a mentor.
44. When engaging with others, always give a compliment or say something positive.

45. Trust your gut.
46. Seize the moment.
47. Have empathy and give people grace: everyone is going through something.
48. Learn how to motivate others.
49. Progress every day.
50. Be proactive.

Bibliography

Angelou, Maya. *Conversations with Maya Angelou*. Edited by Jeffrey M. Elliot. Jackson: University Press of Mississippi, 1989.

Aristotle. *De Anima*. Translated by Hugh Lawson-Tancred. London: Penguin Classics, 1987.

Assael, Shaun, and Mike Mooneyham. *Sex, Lies, and Headlocks: The Real Story of Vince McMahon and the World Wrestling Entertainment*. New York: Crown, 2002.

Barnes, Brooks. "How Dwayne Johnson Became America's Movie Star." *The New York Times*. July 20, 2019.

Barnes, Fred. "Gilbert Arenas: The Assassin." *washingtonian. com*. November 1, 2006. https://www.washingtonian.com/2006/11/01/gilbert-arenas-the-assassin/.

Beaumont-Thomas, Ben. "How did Bad Bunny become the world's biggest pop star?." *The Guardian*, December 4, 2020. https://www.theguardian.com/music/2020/dec/04/how-did-bad-bunny-become-the-worlds-biggest-pop-star.

Belsky, Scott. *Making Ideas Happen: Overcoming the Obstacles Between Vision and Reality*. New York: Portfolio, 2010.

Brandt, Richard L. *One Click: Jeff Bezos and the Rise of Amazon.com*. New York: Portfolio, 2011.

Branson, Richard. *Finding My Virginity: The New Autobiography*. New York: Portfolio/Penguin, 2017.

Branson, Richard. *Losing My Virginity: How I Survived, Had Fun, and Made a Fortune Doing Business My Way*. New York: Crown Business, 1998.

Brown, Judith M. *Gandhi: Prisoner of Hope*. New Haven: Yale University Press, 1991.

Butler, Susan. *East to the Dawn: The Life of Amelia Earhart*. Cambridge, MA: Da Capo Press, 1997.

Canfield, Jack. *The Success Principles: How to Get from Where You Are to Where You Want to Be*. New York: Mariner Books, 2005.

Carmon, Irin, and Shana Knizhnik. *Notorious RBG: The Life and Times of Ruth Bader Ginsburg*. New York: Dey Street Books, 2015.

Chuba, Kirsten. "Jimmy Kimmel to Host Selena Gomez's Third Annual Rare Impact Fund Benefit." *The Hollywood Reporter*, September 10, 2025. https://www.hollywoodreporter.com/lifestyle/lifestyle-news/jimmy-kimmel-selena-gomez-rare-impact-fund-benefit-1236365492/.

Clarey, Christopher. "In Comebacks, Serena Williams Showed ' You Can Never Underestimate Her.'" *The New York Times*. Sept, 2022. https://www.nytimes.com/2022/08/29/sports/tennis/serena-williams-comebacks-us-open.html.

Clarey, Christopher. *The Master: The Brilliant Career of Roger Federer*. New York: Twelve, 2021.

Clarke, Liz. "Serena Williams Outlasts Victoria Azarenka to Claim U.S. Open Women's Title." *The Washington Post*. September 8, 2013. https://www.washingtonpost.com/sports/othersports/serena-williams-outlasts-victoria-azarenka-to-claim-us-open-womens-title/2013/09/08/8c099952-18e5-11e3-a628-7e6dde8f889d_story.html.

Covey, Stephen R. *The 7 Habits of Highly Effective People.* New York: Free Press, 1989.

Covey, Stephen R. *The 7 Habits of Highly Effective People: Powerful Lessons in Personal Change.* New York: Free Press, 1989.

De La Cruz Bobby. "Looking Back at the Fight That Started It All: The Pacquiao-Ledwaba Fight." Accessed June 21, 2021. https://www.boxing247.com/boxing-news/looking-back-at-the-fight-that-started-it-all-the-pacquiao-ledwaba-fight/181017.

Dweck, Carol S. *Mindset: The New Psychology of Success.* New York: Ballantine Books, 2006.

Earhart, Amelia. *The Fun of It.* Chicago: Academy Chicago Publishers, 2006 [1932].

Eker, T. Harv. *Secrets of the Millionaire Mind: Mastering the Inner Game of Wealth.* New York: HarperBusiness, 2005.

Ferriss, Timothy. *Tools of Titans: The Tactics, Routines, and Habits of Billionaires, Icons, and World-Class Performers.* Boston: Houghton Mifflin Harcourt, 2016.

Forbes, B.C. *America's 50 Foremost Business Leaders.* New York: B.C. Forbes and Sons, 1948.

Frankl, Viktor E. *Man's Search for Meaning.* Translated by Ilse Lasch. Boston: Beacon Press, 2006.

Franklin, Benjamin. *The Autobiography of Benjamin Franklin.* Edited by Leonard W. Labaree. New Haven: Yale University Press, 1964.

Gaddis, John Lewis. *The Cold War: A New History.* New York: Penguin Books, 2005.

Gladwell, Malcolm. *Outliers: The Story of Success.* New York: Little, Brown and Company, 2008.

Goggins, David. *Can't Hurt Me: Master Your Mind and Defy the Odds.* New York: Lioncrest Publishing, 2018.

Gregorek, Jerzy and Aniela Gregorek. *The Happy Body: The Simple Science of Nutrition, Exercise, and Relaxation.* Los Altos, CA: Jurania Press, 2010.

Guynn, Jessica. "Mark Zuckerberg Says Steve Jobs Advised Him on Facebook." *Phys*, November 8, 2011.

Hall, Dan. "Inside Matrix Star Keanu Reeves' Tragic Life after Girlfriend's Freak Death and Baby Heartbreak – Before He Found Love." *The Sun*, December 22, 2021. https://www.the-sun.com/entertainment/4321803/keanu-reeves-matrix-resurrections-tragic-life/.

Hamilton, Bethany. "Bethany Hamilton Speaks: Overcoming Obstacles." Motivational Talk. Accessed August 20, 2025. https://bethanyhamilton.com.

Hamilton, Bethany. *Body and Soul: A Girl's Guide to a Fit, Fun and Fabulous Life.* New York: Zondervan, 2014.

Hamilton, Bethany. *Soul Surfer: A True Story of Faith, Family, and Fighting to Get Back on the Board.* New York: MTV Books, 2004.

Hartnett, Mary, and Wendy W. Williams. *Ruth Bader Ginsburg: A Life.* New York: Simon & Schuster, 2018.

Henson, Mike. "Wimbledon 2012: Serena Williams Wins Fifth Singles Title." *BBC.* July 7, 2012. https://www.bbc.com/sport/tennis/18749540

Herrmann, Dorothy. *Helen Keller: A Life.* Chicago: University of Chicago Press, 1999.

Hobson, Nick. "Up at 3:45 a.m., in Bed by 8:45 p.m.: How Apple's CEO Tim Cook Uses Energy Rituals to Optimize His Life." *Inc.* July 4, 2022 https://www.inc.com/nick-hobson/up-at-345am-in-bed-by-845pm-how-apples-ceo-tim-cook-uses-energy-rituals-to-optimize-his-life.html.

Hollingsworth, Amy. *The Simple Faith of Mister Rogers.* Nashville: Thomas Nelson, 2005.

Isaacson, Walter. *Steve Jobs*. New York: Simon & Schuster, 2011.

Johnson, Dwayne, and Joe Layden. *The Rock Says . . . .* New York: HarperCollins, 2000.

Justich, Kerry. "Kevin Hart Reflects on How 2019 Car Accident Changed Him." *Yahoo*, January 9, 2023. https://www.yahoo.com/lifestyle/kevin-hart-2019-car-accident-changed-him-213555785.html.

Kaling, Mindy. *Is Everyone Hanging Out without Me? (And Other Concerns)*. New York: Crown Publishing, 2011.

Kaplan, Sarah. "Meet Katie Bouman, One Woman Who Helped Make the World's First Black Hole Image." *The Washington Post*. April 10, 2019. https://www.washingtonpost.com/science/2019/04/10/see-black-hole-first-time-images-event-horizon-telescope/.

Keller, Helen. *The Story of My Life*. New York: Doubleday, Page & Company, 1903.

King, Martin Luther, Jr. *Why We Can't Wait*. New York: Harper & Row, 1964.

King, Maxwell. *The Good Neighbor: The Life and Work of Fred Rogers*. New York: Abrams Press, 2018.

Krishnamurti, Jiddu. *The First and Last Freedom*. San Francisco: Harper, 1954.

Kondo, Marie. *The Life-Changing Magic of Tidying Up: The Japanese Art of Decluttering and Organizing*. New York: Ten Speed Press, 2014.

Lansky, Sam. "How DJ Khaled Became the Self-Help Sage of Snapchat." *Time*. May 5, 2016. https://time.com/4319116/dj-khaled-snapchat/

Lashinsky, Adam. *Inside Apple: How America's Most Admired—and Secretive—Company Really Works*. New York: Business Plus, 2012.

Lazenby, Roland. *Michael Jordan: The Life*. New York: Little, Brown and Company, 2014.

Lloyd, Jonathan. "Nov. 7, 1991: Magic Johnson's HIV Announcement." NBC News, November 8, 2017. https://www.nbclosangeles.com/news/local/magic-johnson-hiv-announcement/2105289/.

Lowenstein, Roger. *Buffett: The Making of an American Capitalist*. New York: Random House, 1995.

Macur, Juliet. *Cycle of Lies: The Fall of Lance Armstrong*. New York: Harper, 2014.

Maine, D'Arcy. "Simone Biles Withdraws from Individual All-Around Gymnastics Competition at Tokyo Olympics to Focus on Mental Well-Being." *ESPN*. July 28, 2021. https://www.espn.com/olympics/gymnastics/story/_/id/31902290/simone-biles-withdraws-individual-all-competition-tokyo-olympics-focus-mental-health.

Marable, Manning. *Malcolm X: A Life of Reinvention*. New York: Penguin Books, 2011.

McEvoy, Jemima. "Keeping Up with the Kardashians: Meet the Woman Who Made a Fortune Helping Build the Family's Billion-Dollar Business Empire." *Forbes*. June 14, 2022. https://www.forbes.com.

Mervosh, Sarah. "Katie Bouman: The Woman Behind the First Black Hole Image." *The New York Times*. April 11, 2019. https://www.nytimes.com/2019/04/11/science/katie-bouman-black-hole.html.

"Michael Jordan Biography." *Encyclopaedia Britannica*. Updated January 2024. https://www.britannica.com/biography/Michael-Jordan.

Mossburg, Cheri and Marianne Garvey. "Kevin Hart's Wife Says He's 'Going to Be Just Fine.'" *CNN*, September 9, 2019. https://www.cnn.com/2019/09/01/entertainment/kevin-hart-car-crash.

Rare Beauty. "Our Mission." Accessed August 20, 2025. https://rarebeauty.com/pages/rare-impact.

Phelps, Michael, and Alan Abrahamson. *No Limits: The Will to Succeed*. New York: Free Press, 2008.

Robbins, Tony. *Awaken the Giant Within: How to Take Immediate Control of Your Mental, Emotional, Physical, and Financial Destiny!* New York: Simon & Schuster, 1991.

Robbins, Tony. *Unlimited Power: The New Science of Personal Achievement*. New York: Free Press, 1986.

Rosen, Jeffrey. *Conversations with RBG: Ruth Bader Ginsburg on Life, Love, Liberty, and Law*. New York: Henry Holt and Co., 2019.

Rossman, John. *Think Like Amazon: 50 1/2 Ideas to Become a Digital Leader*. New York: McGraw-Hill Education, 2019.

Rūmī, Jalāl al-Dīn. *The Essential Rumi*. Translated by Coleman Barks. San Francisco: HarperCollins, 1995.

BBC News. "Ryan Reynolds & Rob McElhenney: Hollywood Stars' Wrexham Takeover Approved." *BBC*, February 5, 2021.

Schlender, Brent, and Rick Tetzeli. *Becoming Steve Jobs: The Evolution of a Reckless Upstart into a Visionary Leader*. New York: Crown Currency, 2015.

Schroeder, Alice. *The Snowball: Warren Buffett and the Business of Life*. New York: Bantam Books, 2008.

Schultz, Howard, and Joanne Gordon. *Onward: How Starbucks Fought for Its Life without Losing Its Soul*. New York: Rodale, 2011.

Schultz, Howard, and Dori Jones Yang. *Pour Your Heart Into It: How Starbucks Built a Company One Cup at a Time*. New York: Hyperion, 1997.

Seneca, Lucias Annaeus. *Letters from a Stoic*. Translated by Robin Campbell. London: Penguin Classics, 1969.

Shetty, Jay. *Think Like a Monk: Train Your Mind for Peace and Purpose Every Day*. New York: Simon & Schuster, 2020.

Smith, Rory. "Welcome to Wrexham: It's the Future." *New York Times*, September 19, 2022.

Smith, Sam. *The Jordan Rules: The Inside Story of a Turbulent Season with Michael Jordan and the Chicago Bulls*. New York: Pocket Books, 1993.

Smith, Sean. *J. K. Rowling: A Biography*. London: Michael O'Mara Books, 2001.

Stone, Brad. *Amazon Unbound: Jeff Bezos and the Invention of a Global Empire*. New York: Simon & Schuster, 2021.

Stone, Brad. *The Everything Store: Jeff Bezos and the Age of Amazon*. New York: Little, Brown and Company, 2013.

Tidying Up with Marie Kondo. Netflix, 2019.

Valby, Karen. "Everyone Wants a Piece of Pedro Pascal." *Vanity Fair*, June 2025. https://www.vanityfair.com/hollywood/story/pedro-pascal-cover-story?srsltid= AfmBOoo_ Tz3CmleALsgOZQBH3PGx CY0b6a7fRuGQezxg2WqOMu5MS3J0.

Biography.com Editors. "Vera Wang." *Biography*. Last modified April 2, 2014. https://www.biography.com/fashion-designer/vera-wang.

Winfrey, Oprah. *Oprah and Lance Armstrong: The Worldwide Exclusive*. OWN, January 17, 2013. Television broadcast.

Winfrey, Oprah. *The Path Made Clear: Discovering Your Life's Direction and Purpose*. New York: Flatiron Books, 2019.

X, Malcolm and Alex Haley. *The Autobiography of Malcolm X: As Told to Alex Haley*. New York: Ballantine Books, 1964.